There Are No Problem Horses
— Only Problem Riders

Books by Mary Twelveponies

Ride and Learn

Everyday Training: Backyard Dressage

There Are No Problem Horses —
Only Problem Riders

There Are No Problem Horses

Only Problem Riders

MARY TWELVEPONIES

Houghton Mifflin Company Boston
1982

Copyright © 1982 by Mary Cleveland

Library of Congress Cataloging in Publication Data

Twelveponies, Mary.
  There are no problem horses—only problem riders.
  1. Horse-training.   2. Horsemanship.   3. Horses—
Behavior.   I. Title.
SF287.T977 1982   798.2'3   82-12074
ISBN 0-395-32053-4
ISBN 0-395-33194-3 pbk.

Printed in the United States of America

V 10 9 8 7 6 5 4 3 2 1

Portions of this material appeared
previously in *Horse and Horseman*.

For all riders who seek answers
to their horse problems
and for all horses who hope
their riders will find
the correct answers.

Come unto me,
all ye that labor
and are heavy laden,
and I will give you rest.
— MATTHEW 11:28

Contents

Author's Note

When my daughter suggested that — because of my success in analyzing and prescribing cures of horse problems personally — I should write a letter-answering column on the subject, I was quite hesitant. I wouldn't be able to see the horses and how their riders handled them, so I was fearful of giving bad advice. After a year of study and reading some existing columns that offered not only poor but dangerous advice, I decided to give it a try.

No one can know all the answers, but the high degree of success my readers have had with the solutions I've offered them gives me confidence that the advice I give you here is good and true. The highly experienced horse handler may have some methods that are quicker — I do myself in some cases — but safety is of the utmost importance. Some shortcuts which I would never use myself are dangerous to both the horse and the handler. Others require skill in handling ropes and other equipment that would be difficult, and even dangerous, to learn except in personal, on-the-job training.

For these reasons I offer solutions based not on merely subduing the horse, but instead on utilizing the way he thinks and is capable of moving and learning. Because the latter approach is the sound foundation of all good horse handling, it makes subsequent training easier and less problem-provoking — the proverbial ounce of prevention.

May you all be successful with your horses and all your horses be happy.

Mary Twelveponies

Poor Iam! I'm at fault for trying to force the pivot without balancing him to the rear.

Now I do everything right and Iam starts around in a beautiful pivot.

Introduction: Why We Have Problem Horses

When pride rideth in the saddle, destruction rideth on the crupper.

— *Unknown*

It is the hardest pill for all of us would-be horsemen to swallow, but it is absolutely true — if the horse is not responding properly, we are doing something wrong. Sure, basic physical problems such as poor conformation or a nervous disposition can make a horse difficult to train. Or emotional problems brought on by previous experiences can cause difficulties. But there is a true solution to every problem and it is up to us to find out what that solution is and use it wisely.

If we don't know or understand the basic principles of correct riding and training, we can be committing gross errors. If we are highly skilled and educated in the art of horsemanship, we can still make mistakes in the way we apply the basics to any individual horse. If a horse steps on your foot on purpose, it's your fault for having your foot in his way. If he does it a second time, it's your fault for not being quick enough and firm enough with punishment the first time. This is a highly simplified example and it could give you the wrong impression — the idea that everything the horse does wrong should be punished immediately.

Punishment, however, is not the answer in most points of finer riding. If your horse doesn't turn a corner properly, stop and ask yourself what you did wrong that he didn't understand what you meant by a proper corner. If a horse is capable of doing what you ask, it is up to you to ask in such a way that he will do it. Once you understand that the answer to your horse's problems is in finding your own mistakes, you are on your way to finding the correct solutions.

Before we talk about solutions, let's talk about causes in general. I think one of the biggest reasons people end up with problem horses is pride of ownership. The horse has always been a status symbol. In the days when he was the principal means of transportation, status was proclaimed by owning the Cadillacs in horses, leaving the Chevies and Fords to the lower classes. This class-linked symbolism has carried over to present times when owning horses for sport is no longer reserved for kings. Now many people want to own the classy, "spirited" show horses to prove they are kings of the sport.

Parents are often the worst offenders. They want the "best" for their kids — not necessarily the best for the kids' own good, but the best for their own vanity so they can say to friends and neighbors, "Look how well my kid can ride that good-looking, spirited horse!" Too often it's like telling the kids to go play on the freeway. I remember when I was about ten years old and still longing fruitlessly for a pony, a neighbor bought his daughter a palomino pinto pony, complete with show harness and cart. The whole outfit was beautiful — the pony a large, show-trained one with a spanking trot. While I stood by with that green gleam in my eyes and the daughter stood by timidly watching, the father proudly hitched up the pony for her to drive. I am sure she didn't drive or ride that pony more than a dozen times total. She was a young girl — not a brave or experienced horsewoman — and the pony's brisk gaits were more than her nerves could stand. But her father had wanted the pony-to-be-proud-of. This is the stuff problems are made of, and grownups often make the same kind of mistake when buying horses for themselves.

One of the most "beautiful" horses I ever saw looked just like a woolly mammoth. It was in one of my classes in early spring — there she stood, with thick yellow fur swirling all over her body in curls and coils. Hair four inches long or more cloaked her legs in ruffled pantaloons. She looked just like a walking stuffed animal toy. My other students couldn't help laughing, which

Beneath this woolly coat beats a heart of gold. Sugar Babe's disposition makes up for what she lacks in looks.

started her owner apologizing in a very loving tone of voice. Lots of horses do look funny in their winter coats, but this one was unique. I marveled at her unusual appearance, yet to me her most outstanding features were her large, quiet eyes and her very tractable manner as we all closed in on her to massage loose great globs of her shedding wool. Her owner confirmed what I saw, that she was a very dependable saddle horse.

Mutual trust between horse and rider is important. I mentioned the neighbor girl's timidity with the show pony. All degrees of fear of horses can cause problems with the horse, and the horse that is too much for you to handle can cause the fear problem to develop in you. It's not that the horse is basically out to get you but that he is a lazy thing, with more or less subtle ways of trying to get his own way. Later I will go into the problems horses have with timid and fearful riders and what those riders can do about their trepidations.

You can get a well-trained horse that matches your riding ability and still have problems crop up. One of the biggest causes is just plain not riding the horse enough. It is just a simple matter of riding your horse regularly to keep him in the habit of obedience. If he spends weeks or months in his stable or corral, his responses get rusty and he is inclined to want to go his own way. After ten minutes of steady trotting in my riding classes, even the flighty horses are relaxed and ready to go to work, regardless of their riders' capabilities. It's the same old wet-saddle-blanket rule.

Another reason people get problem horses is what I call the

"Wild West Syndrome." This is the tradition-pressure that it is un-American to be unable to ride, even if you have only seen horses on TV. Thus you get people who think of themselves as able to ride and train anything with hair, so they get themselves or their kids a colt to "raise and train the way they want it trained." Riding and training both take knowledge and skill; so whether they buy a colt or a fancy horse, these people soon find themselves with a hooligan by the halter.

Part of the Wild West Syndrome is the do-it-or-else training method. This works fine until the person runs into a horse that rebels or until the person wants a higher degree of perfection in his horses. While a trainer of this type who is successful within his limited sphere has a lot to be proud of, he will have to swallow his pride in order to improve his product. The thinking trainer learns (sooner or later) that it isn't just a case of finding more ways of forcing the horse into obedience — it's a case of retraining himself so his horses can respond better. Success and traditional training methods can be barriers to more learning. After all, if you are winning, it hurts to admit you might need a tune-up or a complete overhaul instead of a minor adjustment to improve your horse's performance.

Another reason you can end up with problems is ignoring the silk-purse proverb. You don't stop to consider that this horse that is giving you trouble with fancy show training may not be physically, mentally, or emotionally capable of the job you are asking

Pi Dough is a good "usin' pony" but not "silk purse" material. Problems can develop from unrealistic expectations.

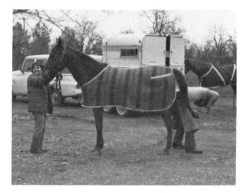

Sometimes the best solution is to pull the horse's shoes and nail them on another horse.

him to do. Then there is mechanization. You think, "A horse is a horse. How could there be a personality conflict between him and me?" All horses have the common denominator of basic instincts, but every horse is an individual. Before you spur and quirt the obstinate beast into submission, let us reason together to find the cause and thus the cure for your individual problem.

I have had some people write asking for help with a horse that has so many problems it would take a whole book — this one — to tell them how to cure them all. These people usually close the letter with "Please help. I love him too much to sell him." This isn't true love — this is just being proud of a beautiful beast or being too proud to admit a mistaken choice. As I said in the beginning, there is a solution for every problem; but in some cases the best one is to pull the horse's shoes and nail them on another horse.

There is no need to be hasty about picking this solution. The nervous horse may need worming and vitamins. The emotionally abused horse may respond to patient, understanding, correct handling. Proper training exercises can overcome conformation problems to a great extent. Whether or not you dispose of the horse depends on how much time you are willing to spend, how realistic you want to be about the best work you can get from him, and how satisfied you will be with that kind of work.

There are lots of good horses, many of them needing good homes, so you need to decide if you really want to put in the hours and sweat needed to rehabilitate the horse you now have.

If you are convinced that no one else would give him a good home or you are squeamish about consigning him to the fate of Jezebel, then you are probably stuck with all that work and worry. But if the horse is quite dangerous to handle, think twice about keeping him. Your life and limbs are more precious than any single horse.

I myself have given up on a few horses — most of them back in the days when I knew far less than I do now. Just recently, though, I gave up on one simply because I could not make myself face all that hard work needed to overcome his physical problems and to undo the mistakes I had made with him. That horse was Dos Reales, and you will be hearing more about him from time to time. Dos is a horse that is built with a high head and a low back. That makes more work in training, since the first step is to get a horse's head down and his back up, so he can step under with his hind legs. No horse can balance himself and later collect himself until he steps under behind.

Dos had discovered that he could run away with his first handler — both under saddle and out of the longe circle. He is not mean in any way but very smart, so he coolly used this trick against me. He also showed a distinct preference for my husband, Bill, but I owned him so I thought he should be mine . . . don't you agree? No, we have to be realistic. Although I did make a lot of progress with Dos, it took a lot of work and a lot of learning. He is happy now doing what he likes to do — being Bill's pleasure horse. Horses have their druthers, too.

In this book, I will tell you all the solutions I know for the problems that you may come across. Some people say that the right answer depends on which expert you ask. The solutions I will give you are all techniques that I have used successfully. In some cases I can tell you things I have tried and found wanting and things I have read about that shouldn't ever be tried. I will put in a few ounces of prevention, too, as well as the pounds of cure. If you can recognize a problem's early symptoms, you can save yourself and your horse a lot of misery.

I have had a few people say that what I've told them doesn't work. They have seen me and my friends make it work on their horses; they have even made it work on their horses themselves

Dos Reales's natural high head–low back combination makes it harder to train him correctly, yet his good qualities make him worth the work for the right person.

under our instruction. Yet these riders immediately go back to their old ways when "Teach" can't be watching. Whether they lack understanding or the desire to improve or are too proud to admit that they need to improve their riding, I don't know. I do know that a solution won't work if you don't use it. Even though it is work at first to substitute good habits for bad ones, it is worth it for the greater pleasure — and safety — you will get out of your horse. All I can do is tell you the solution. It is up to you to develop the ability to apply it.

In my book *Everyday Training: Backyard Dressage* I have gone into detail on the way to sit on a horse properly and aid him properly. "Properly" in my book is "the easiest way to get the best results." If you want to get the most out of this problem horse material, you should read *Everyday Training* and put those ideas into practice. The basic skills you will learn will make it much easier for you to apply the solutions I am offering you here.

Of course, if you feel that that is too much like work, you can always keep getting another horse, which you will find soon develops the same problems your last one had. There are no problem horses — only problem riders.

PART I

Basics

*Wisdom is the principal thing;
therefore, get wisdom; and with all
thy getting, get understanding.*
—PROVERBS 4:7

1

Communication

Learning the horse's language

Curing a horse's problems is simply a matter of backing up and retraining him the way it should have been done in the first place — a matter of replacing bad habits with good ones. The trouble is that retraining a horse is four or five times harder than doing it right in the first place. In the most severe cases some emergency measures are necessary, but mostly it is a case of staying alert to be ahead of the horse in every move he makes so you can use the proper aids to get the proper response and then give him the proper reward. This is good communication.

Poor communication is one of the main reasons so many horses today develop bad habits (other than the fact that many of them just aren't ridden enough). So many people nowadays don't know how to "read" a horse. I guess they are so used to a mechanized world that they don't think about a horse having ideas of his own. But the knack for understanding horses is a talent some are born with; and, if they are around horses and horse people, a talent they develop rapidly; practically by osmosis. Others must try harder. But everyone can learn to "read" a horse — and should, if he is serious about becoming a good rider.

To be able to handle a horse well, you must be able to understand his language so you can listen to him intelligently. If you know what the horse is saying to you, you will know what you must say to him and how to say it to get the results you want. When listening and reacting have become reflex actions, your aids will be timely and effective. An aid applied too late is not only ineffective — it can mean an entirely different thing to the horse in some cases. You can't send the horse to his bedroom with the threat, "Just wait until your father gets home!" You have to tell him now!

I can help you some with the horse's language, but you will have to help yourselves from there on by studying your horses at all times possible. Observe their expressions — throughout their whole bodies — and the actions that follow. By watching every movement, small and large, of a horse's head, body, feet, and tail, and noticing what he or the horse near him does next, you can learn what the horse is thinking about doing. This will help you understand what he will think about doing in a given situation. You will be able to see some of these expressions when you are mounted; others you will have to learn to feel. This is the only way you will ever learn to be responsive soon enough to train a horse.

There are several reports out now on studies of horse behavior. The ones I have seen all deal with the horse's basic instincts and try to be scientifically objective. But we are not interested in being scientific. We are interested in being able to understand the horse in his present environment, which includes his living quarters and the animals and people around him. Instincts are just the beginning of such understanding. We are interested in horses' thoughts, movements, and reactions, so we can learn to tell the horse which movement we want, when, and how.

By observing horses' actions and expressions, you can learn to "read" their thoughts and begin to develop a feel for their actions under saddle. This will help you anticipate and prevent misbehavior and encourage good behavior.

Whenever I am training a horse, I study him while he's running loose as well as when he's being handled. I notice his eyes, because they do have expression in them. It is important to understand those expressions in order to be able to proceed intelligently with his training. You can see a wide variety of expressions: A horse can glare in anger and can show fright in his eyes. Bill's blue-eyed pinto was especially good at glaring, usually at me. When I finally found Pi Dough, who had gotten lost in the brush, he was so scared his eyes were glazed. He didn't see me or hear me, even though I was walking and talking out in the open not 25 feet from him. I was quite relieved that he did hear and recognize the sound of grain in the bucket because he was just walking away from me in a daze. It only took one glance at his eyes to know he was almost totally out of it, and his actions matched his expression.

A horse's eyes can look soft, showing relaxation and willingness. They can have worry lines over them, which indicates lack of understanding or anxiety about what you are doing to the horse, or asking him to do. If those worry lines are there constantly, even when the horse is not being handled, they can indicate a nervous disposition or a health problem. Some horses use the famous Thelwell "hooded look" a lot, but I have never seen a horse follow through on that look with anything that would indicate a sinister meaning. It is the actions that accompany each look that tell you its meaning — not the imaginings of your mind.

Horses can pinpoint their gaze with a bright look in their eyes or they can get a faraway, disinterested look. I have seen two horses switch back and forth between these expressions for several minutes. At the end of class one night Mary was talking to me while holding her mare, Rena. We happened to be standing near the coffee table, so Rena's head was within a foot or so of it. The mare had been worked hard and was resting with her head lowered. As I talked, I noticed her roll her eyes toward the table with a bright, interested look. She would hold it for half a second and then roll her eyes away to a disinterested stare. She did this two or three times before I called everyone's attention to it, and still she continued to do it. Her head never moved (although her

The Thelwell "hooded look." Tyke is simply waiting for a carrot here. It's the actions that follow an expression that teach you what it means.

ears may have), but it was her eyes that drew our attention. Mary finally decided that Rena could smell the sugar and that was what interested her, but she is not the overbearing type that takes what isn't offered.

The other occasion was one time when my horse Dos had his head through the barn window while I was mixing his grain. You know how you get the feeling that someone is staring in your direction. I felt this and looked up to see Dos's bright eyes fastened on the grain-mixing procedure. When I looked at him, he immediately turned his eyes away with that faraway stare. As soon as I looked down at the grain, he again turned his bright-eyed gaze on it. It took me quite a while to mix that feeding because I kept looking from Dos to the grain and back again just to watch his eyes change expression and focus. Dos is a bashful horse that dislikes very much being looked straight in the eye.

This brings me to an important point. Only on rare occasions and for specific reasons should you ever look a horse straight in the eye. Hardly any horse likes it, although most of them are not quite as bashful as Dos. You can check a horse's expression with a quick glance or watch it out of the corner of your eye. A horse's eye expression is very important — it is the first thing I check when I approach a horse. I check it often while I am handling him from the ground and whenever the horse turns his head while I am on him. It helps me tell whether he is relaxed and asleep or relaxed and willing; tense and angry or tense and frightened; and whether he is thinking or spaced out. But I don't read complicated human thoughts into the expressions I see — just horse thoughts that I know are there because of horse actions I have seen accompany the expressions repeatedly.

From eyes we go to ears. The scientific researchers usually claim that all of the horse's expression is in the ears, but I know for a fact that I check the eyes alone as often as I check the ears alone. Actually, the eyes, ears, lips and attitude of the head all tie in together and I make my final "diagnosis" in a critical case by putting them all together. The way the ears are set on, along with other features of the head, can tell you a lot about an individual horse's disposition. Ears set high and to the front of the head, usually close together, indicate a nervous, flighty horse — even more so if he is hawk-faced with round eyes set on the side. Ears lopped out to each side indicate a sullen horse, and when any horse lops his ears out and down, beware of what he does next: It is an indication that he is figuring out how to retaliate.

If you handle a lot of different horses and make a habit of studying the shape and expressions of their heads, you can learn a lot. Some trainers can even read a horse's basic personality without having to handle him to find out. This takes lots of experience. You can learn a little about a horse's personality just by asking each horse's handler, but that is very difficult because

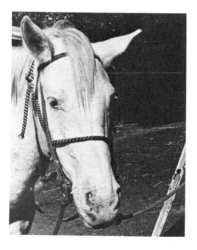

The lop-eared horse can be sullen and inclined to fight to the finish. He requires very tactful handling.

some people think all horses are kind kiddies that can be bribed into good behavior with treats. Others think all horses are stubborn things that are always out to defy them. Both types of people create problem horses — the first by lack of discipline, the second by starting fights. Somewhere in between are the thinking horsemen who study horses and can help you learn how to understand them.

Back to the ears, which are so obvious that you have heard all about them: pricked at attention; turned back — one ear or both — listening to the rear; and laid back flat, indicating threat or anger. There are some horses who greet you with their ears laid back. Dos is one of these, and my colt, Iam, has picked it up from him. These ears are not plastered tight to the horse's head the way an angry horse's ears are, and the side to side head motion is missing as well as the glare in the eyes. Dos's eyes have a "don't touch" look but Iam's are just there. While there is a definite difference in overall expression between the pinned-back, angry ears and the ones that are laid back as a greeting, I never go up to a strange horse who lays his ears back as I approach. If he wants to be unsociable, I will accommodate him — unless I have to catch him. In that case, I will walk up to him confidently and calmly while I watch for any signs of aggression in him. Ears are

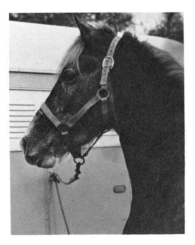

Smoki's head and expression indicate that he is smart, direct-minded and willing; but he will step on you and crowd you if you let him. He will also get mad at unjust punishment.

so mobile and visible from so many angles that they are a very important clue to a horse's attitude.

A horse's lips can indicate his mood, all the way from the total relaxation of a hanging lower lip to the tension or anger of tightly clamped lips. I knew one horse named Coltburger who would even stick his upper lip down stiffly in a pout at times during training. (I recently ran across another horse that would do this too.) This pout indicates the horse feels unjustly or overly punished, and such a horse may retaliate. In short, he has a short temper. When I see that pout, I immediately get the horse to do something I can praise him for so he can relax. You can't teach an angry horse anything except that you are the boss.

A relaxed horse will usually have closed, relaxed lips, but some horses will pop their lower lip in rhythm with their work when they're relaxed. If the popping is quite rapid, the horse is not relaxed. Tight lips with wrinkles around them indicate tension. The circumstances will tell you whether the horse just isn't relaxed yet, doesn't understand or isn't capable of what you are asking, or is angry.

A horse expresses his thoughts by a wide range of movements. Henry Blake, in his book *Talking With Horses*, describes the way a horse can swing his head to tell you to get back in line because he is boss. A horse can also indicate bossiness by giving you a shove with his body or shoulder, but if he stays crowded against you, he is either disrespectful, ignoring your presence, or may be frightened and seeking your warm side just as he would his mother's when he was a foal.

A horse that moves his head from side to side as you approach from the rear is a nervous horse. If he also has his tail clamped and his haunches sucked under, he plans to defend himself by kicking if he feels it is necessary. A horse will first clamp his tail and drop his haunches when something gooses him into bucking or bolting. This is a physical move to mobilize his forces for the move that follows. That's how we get the term "grab his tail" — a move that calls for instant reaction on the part of the rider to control the situation (see p. 31).

Horses talk to other horses through body movements. We can see a lot of these movements and learn to understand them by

Iam's pricked ears and intense eyes indicate that he is ignoring his rider.

watching the reactions of the other horses. Some of these movements are so subtle that we don't see them. I remember the time my husband Bill was going to pony me on my Frosty filly to get her started under saddle. She had never been ponied before, so I asked him to lead her around some with his horse, Patches, before I got on. He took his dallies on the saddle horn and started off, but Frosty immediately pulled back violently and threw herself. He tried several times with the same results. I couldn't see what the problem was, so I asked Bill if I could try. The moment I got settled in the saddle and asked Patches to move, I felt it.

The stiffness of these turned-back ears and the staring eye show that Iam isn't relaxed.

Add a twist or toss of the head and you know the horse is resisting his rider.

There wasn't any outward sign — no flattening of the ears, no movement of his head — but I could feel him threaten Frosty. I don't know what I felt and don't know why Patches felt he should threaten her, but Frosty was so scared of him from whatever he did that we had to give up on the ponying.

Horses can communicate other feelings with movements of the tail and feet. The swishing tail that says there's a fly biting the horse on his rump is slightly different from the swishing tail that says he is mad enough to kick you at any moment. The foot cocked at rest looks different from the foot cocked in readiness for a kick. More aggressively, the horse may give you one big swipe with his tail as you walk by or work around him. This is to warn you about things such as invading his privacy or grooming him too roughly or tightening the cinch too suddenly or too much. Horses sometimes lift a foot in a threatening manner or even kick it through the air beside you. The lifted-foot threat doesn't call for overreaction on your part — just a firm verbal reprimand. The kick, however, calls for a swift swat on the side of his belly. At times we shouldn't spare the rod, but we should not overdo it.

You must translate all the nuances of expression you have seen on the ground into what you feel when you are on his back. That is the one big secret of expert horsemanship — listening to what the horse says. If you don't know what he is going to do, you can't encourage or discourage it.

You have to "listen" while you are working a horse to see if he

The relaxed, cooperative horse carries both ears turned back relaxed and listening, occasionally flicking one or both forward for a moment. His eyes are soft.

understands, if he is able to do what you ask, or if he just plain doesn't want to do it. If the feedback is positive, you know you can continue what you are doing and make progress. If you get negative feedback, you need to back up and think about what needs to be done next. You can't just bludgeon a horse into obedience and hope to get the best results. You have to listen to the horse's side of the story, too.

There is another very good reason for studying horses other than being able to read them accurately. If you are going to teach a horse anything, you have to be able to explain it to him in his language. Trick horse trainers know this very well. For example, they know that a horse will nod his head up and down at a fly on his breast and that he'll shake it from side to side at a fly biting him on the crest of his neck. By using pin pricks for fly bites and goodies for rewards, they condition the horse's reflexes so he will answer "yes" and "no" to a slight movement of the hand which is unnoticeable to the audience.

Similarly, many horses will move into pressure on the body but will move away from a slap on the same area. When we know this, we can teach the horse to move away from the pressure of our leg by tapping with the whip when we press the leg against his side. Then, by stopping the aids and saying kind words, we reward him and let him know he has understood properly. Soon he is speaking our language — moving away from the leg pressure.

This is the sum total of methodical horse training: Put the

horse in a position where he will respond mentally and physically with the movement desired; apply the proper aids by themselves or with an explanatory aid if necessary; and reward the horse for responding correctly. If he isn't responding correctly, listen to him so you can figure out how to vary the explanation so he will understand you. Then, through careful repetition of each little success, you can turn it into better, more consistent performance and finally into habit. They say that a person hasn't really learned a foreign language until he has learned to think in it. The same thing applies to training a horse. When he has learned to think in your language, then he is really trained.

Becoming the horse's boss

In order to handle a horse successfully, you must establish that you are the boss. This doesn't mean that you should beat a horse into submission. Some people are too rough and others are too easy on a horse. Both types are horse spoilers. To be a horse's true boss and not his tyrannical master, you have to use his language to assert yourself. Horses, like most of God's creatures (including humans) have a pecking order. What you have to do is establish that you are one notch above every horse that you handle.

Some horses are born leaders; others are born to stay at the end of the line. I have known some colts that were so aggressive that my first step in training them would be to call the vet for alterations. I don't consider a horse with this type of disposition to be good stallion material since breeding that kind of horse just propagates inborn disobedience. However, the bold horse that is a leader without being selfishly ambitious makes the best horse for many types of competitions — as long as you are his boss. Keep in mind that all horses from the boldest to the most timid want you to command their respect. On the days that my horse Dos had outsmarted me, at the end of the ride he would stand there beside me, looking off into the distance as if I didn't exist. On the days when I had outsmarted him, he would keep his eyes on me and even nuzzle me, and he isn't a demonstrative horse. Spoiling your horse with sugary love won't make him love you.

Bold horses must be handled firmly, with fair, consistent discipline. (The number one definition of discipline is strict and regular training.) Horses that are "forever yours" must be handled with kindness and understanding so you don't confuse them into rebellion or a nervous breakdown. But no matter what sort of disposition the horse has, you must always stay on top of him. (I have heard that this is the way to ride — just stay on top!) While you must never let any horse discover that he is bigger and stronger than you are, you must train each one intelligently, according to his individual character. All of this takes us right back to understanding horses. If you know how horses think, then you know what they might do — and can guard against the possibility of their doing it even when they look as if they won't. Then you can prevent behavior and accidents that create problems.

How to handle this quick creature that outweighs you eight to ten times is part of the solutions I will give you — how to outthink, outweigh, and outmaneuver him. For each problem and its solutions, I will try to cover enough variations so that each one of you will be able to figure out what is needed for your own special problem child.

2

Basic Training

Training the horse to go forward

The answer to 99 percent of all horse problems is to train the horse to go forward willingly, in a manner that is relaxed and under control. When a horse balks, it is obvious that he is not willing to go forward. Less obvious is the fact that he can't rear, buck, kick, or shy without slowing down first. Stopping, standing, and backing well are dependent upon his willingness to go forward, too. If a horse is dogging along with his emergency brake on, he will be sloppy and slow about stopping. If he isn't willing to move on, he won't stand at attention or step back freely and precisely. So the prevention and cure of problems starts with teaching the horse to go forward willingly, both mentally and physically — mentally, so you can control his thoughts, and physically, so you can control his actions.

In order to control a horse to prevent bad behavior and to

Iam stands at attention, indicating his willingness to go forward. The ideal round corral helps both to control the horse and to encourage him to go forward willingly.

induce good behavior, first you have to get his attention; and it doesn't pay to get it with a two-by-four. In order to teach your horse anything you must keep his mind on his work, so you must keep your mind on your work — not just go along for the ride. You will need to establish your horse's willingness to listen and respond with energy. This doesn't mean that he should jump ahead like a scared jackrabbit or travel in all his gaits with quick choppy steps, because that is a sign that he isn't relaxed. Your ultimate goal is a horse that pays attention and puts more energy into long, relaxed strides every time you close your legs on him to ask him to move. Training or retraining a horse is always work, but once you have established his willingness to go forward as a habit, the rest of the work becomes a pleasure.

Make sure that you start retraining your horse in a place that encourages your horse to pay attention to his work. Distractions will defeat your purpose. You also have to do the initial training in a safe place because you must never let the horse know that he is bigger and stronger than you are. I have found that the safest and best place is a round corral 60 feet in diameter with fencing of poles or boards at least six feet high. It is safest because the horse can't escape — in fact he wouldn't even attempt it — so it physically helps you control him.

Besides that, the psychological effect is right for both you and the horse. You can move him forward because there is no place for him to run away to; and he can move forward because there aren't any corners to get his head stuck in. You also don't have to confuse him by turning him or discourage him by slowing him down excessively. In such a corral you can keep the horse under control without destroying his will to go forward.

It may not be feasible to build this kind of corral just to train or retrain one or two horses, even though it will be useful as both a longeing pen and a place to practice your riding. Except when I was training horses professionally, I have had to do without this ideal training aid, but I always make use of any area confined to 50 or 60 feet each way by fences, buildings, trees, and big brush. Almost any type of fence will do except an electric one or barbed wire. The trees must have branches that are too low for the horse to duck under. Some kind of confinement is necessary because taking a colt or spoiled horse out in the open is inviting trouble.

No matter what you use on a horse's head for control, it will not control him reliably until he learns to accept it. The best way to get the horse to accept it is through education, not through pain. A curb or leverage bit of any kind inflicts enough pain to take the horse's mind off his work, so the proper tool to use for training is the ordinary snaffle with ring cheeks — no leverage shanks — and a broken mouthpiece or a flexible rubber one. (The bosal hackamore is also a proper training tool but it is not easy for most people to use safely, so I won't go into its use here.) Any other bits and gimmicks are just substitutes for knowledge.

You will also need a riding whip to help teach your horse to go forward willingly. It should be long enough and flexible enough to reach the horse's flank behind your leg while your hands are in front of your hips. The right length for most people and horses is about 48 inches, including the short lash. Learn to hold the whip in your fist with the base (not the top) of the handle resting on top of your hand to keep it from slipping. Do not close your little finger on it except to make it flip against the horse's side. That way you can learn to use the whip without jerking on the reins.

Improperly used spurs can cause a horse to slow down or even

The proper way to hold the reins and the 48-inch whip. Close your fingers with a slight twist of the wrist to flick the whip on the horse's side. If you have a shorter whip, let the knob on the end rest on top of your fist.

get balky. Few riders have steady enough legs to be able to avoid spurring a horse when he doesn't need it. So the spurs bang the horse's sides, which makes him spurt forward — which upsets the rider, making him jerk the reins and even spur the horse again. Soon the horse decides that spurring means for him to slow down or stop. The same can be said of the whip if you don't take the time to learn to carry and use it properly. Practice touching the horse with the tip of the whip until you can tell when it contacts him without having to look. Get proficient with it in either hand. If your horse moves forward during practice, praise him; don't stop him.

One other thing on equipment . . . To have the most tactful control of the horse, you should hold the reins between your little and ring fingers, with the ends coming out over the tops of your forefingers. Close your thumbs on top of the reins. The reins should be the right width to fit between the knuckle and first joint of each forefinger with a little bit of friction when your fingers are closed on them. If they are too wide, you cannot close your forefingers on them comfortably. If they are too narrow, you cannot relax your hands without letting them slip. I use a three-quarter-inch width. Try various widths to see what fits your hands, so you can have the best control with the greatest flexibility.

With the snaffle bridle on the horse, the right size reins in your hands, and the whip to reinforce your leg aids, you are ready to ride your horse in the confined area. To tell a horse to move forward, you simply close the insides of your calves on him more firmly. Keep your toes pointed straight ahead and close your calves straight in — never toward the rear. (If you are ever caught without a whip and need to kick, take your lower legs straight out and kick them straight in. Never kick toward the rear because that tips your seat out of the saddle and defeats your purpose.) You don't have to use a lot of pressure when closing your legs. If you don't get a response, either your horse doesn't know what it means or he isn't willing to obey. So relax your legs and close them again, at the same time tapping him with the whip hard enough to make him move. This explains to him what your leg aid means.

Iam is inattentive and ignores my ineffective kick that takes my seat out of the saddle.

A horse will naturally move when hit with the whip, but if you use the whip alone you will always have to carry it. Always give him one chance first to respond just to the leg aid. If he doesn't respond, repeat the leg aid with the explanation he understands — the whip. You always have to find out how hard to use the whip for each individual horse. Otherwise you would teach him that he only has to respond when hit hard, or that being hit means to run away. When I first carried a whip with Dos, I had to hit my boot instead of his side to avoid an over-reaction. Other horses may not feel anything less than a smart crack. Start with a light tap, then a harder one and a harder one until the horse responds. Then you will know how hard to hit initially. When the horse understands that the whip is not something you are petting him with, he will respond to lighter taps or just a touch most of the time.

There are many things that discourage a horse from going forward. Some riders train their horses to piddle along by constantly slowing them down with the reins. But the biggest discouragement comes from the stiff rider with hands that constantly jerk the horse's mouth. Today's style of seat in western equitation must have been invented by a non-rider, because with the rider's heels forced down and the back held stiffly erect, the rider's seat cannot go along with the motion of the horse's back. This stiff, unyielding seat assaults the horse's back and makes him reluctant to move forward willingly.

Unsteady hands go along with a rider who is stiff or insecure. He will be tense in the shoulders and elbows and his hands will bounce and jerk as his body moves. Pretend that you are a horse and that every step forward you take is accompanied by a jerk on your mouth. Or pretend that every time your rider tries to tell you to move better, he drops contact, then jerks your mouth each time he kicks or swats you with the reins or whip. Would *you* be willing to go forward?

You must learn to sit deep and relaxed in the saddle with your upper calves, knees, and thighs closed on the horse, and your feet just resting on the stirrups. You must sit tall with your shoulders back and your head up, looking where you are going. You must stay relaxed in the waist, because any time you stiffen your waist you will slow the horse down. Relax your waist by letting your stomach hang loose while you stretch your body up tall. You must also be relaxed in your shoulders, elbows, and neck. If you will bring your chin in so your face is in the vertical and the curve is out of the back of your neck, it will relax your neck and the rest of your body, too.

Maintain contact with the horse's mouth as you ask him to go forward. Loose reins won't help him go forward any better; in fact, they will make him travel on his forehand and just drag himself around. Then, when you take up on the reins to ask him to turn or slow down, you startle him and make him apprehensive of the rein aids. Make the contact firm with flexible fingers that squeeze shut and gradually relax as needed (see photos). I have lots of trouble getting this idea across to my students. They are so imbued with the notion that light hands make light mouths that they will let a horse practically run away rather than keep a firm enough contact to control the horse. *Light hands leave the contact light when the horse makes it light, and immediately start to relax each time they must be squeezed shut tight; but they are always ready to put the squeeze on again whenever it's needed.*

Another thing I have trouble getting students to do is to ride the trot with their hands on the horse's neck (one on each side, just in front of the withers). You have to take a forward position on the horse's back to do this, bending in your hip joints — not the middle of your back. I ride colts this way, and any rider who has trouble with his hands bouncing should do it. You can control a horse quite well this way — simply by looking where you want to go and squeezing your hands shut and relaxing them as needed — yet rider after rider will raise his hands off the neck the moment he starts trotting forward. One student even told me, "But I'll fall off if I put my hands down!" I couldn't imagine how! When you ride with your hands down, keep a slight bend in your elbows so they can act as shock absorbers. Straight arms tend to lock into position and destroy the rider's feel and flexibility.

When you have told a horse to go forward better, it is essential that you do not immediately tell him to slow down. You don't want him to leap ahead out of control, but you do want him to learn to respond to your legs and the whip. Slowing him down abruptly just because he is moving too fast would punish him for obeying your driving aids. If he hurries off, let him rush for a few strides as you tactfully encourage him to slow his speed without losing his energy.

Along with getting your horse to move, you also want to develop a steady rhythm. In order to do this you must have good feel of the horse and his intentions. If you don't relax your fingers and urge him to go forward just as you feel him start to slow down, he will slow down too much. If you wait until he has slowed down too much and then boot him forward suddenly, he will move in spurts. Get him going and start working subtly for a

Bend forward from your hips, keep your hands on the horse's neck, and keep your elbows slightly bent to avoid jerking the horse's mouth as you train him to trot forward willingly. Here Iam is rhythmic, relaxed, and energetic.

good steady rhythm. Invite the horse to slow his rhythm by gently relaxing your fingers, but be ready to squeeze (not grab) them shut if he wants to rush off. When he does finally drop into a steady rhythm, relaxation comes with it and you are on your way to a horse that truly goes forward willingly.

Every time you ask your horse to walk, you are rewarding him, especially with the walk on loose rein. So keep him trotting forward, tactfully regulating his speed until he settles into longer strides that slow his speed and rhythm. If you trot him for five minutes without getting this relaxed rhythm and stop, thinking "I'll rest him a little and then try again," you are simply rewarding him for rushing around. Trot on until you get the rhythm you want, but remember that jerking the horse's mouth keeps him nervous and rushing. Let him stretch his head forward and down.

If it has been difficult to get this relaxed rhythm, reward your horse as soon as you get it by coaxing him down to a walk and then walking for half a minute on loose rein. Then smoothly take up the reins and work him again. This instant reward system makes a horse happy to comply, but don't try to force it on every horse. My colt, Iam, gave me trouble every day with warming up into the desired rhythm; but when he did get it, he enjoyed it so much that he didn't want to walk. If your horse is easy to get moving with the long, relaxed strides, let him trot on for about

Iam stretches his head forward and down and I bend in the hips to "go down with him." This helps the horse relax during his initial training and warm-up.

First get a good, forward walk, then let the horse walk on a long rein like this.

five minutes before rewarding him with the walk. Use the horse's language: He tends to repeat rewarded performance — so reward him *when he is doing what you want*, not what you are trying to cure him of doing.

A word of warning on the loose rein walk. Every time you ask the horse to come down to the walk, make sure he walks forward with energy on contact. When he is walking well, let the reins slip through your fingers so he can stretch his head down, *then* give him loose reins. If you simply drop the reins the moment you come down to the walk, you may teach the horse to jerk them out of your hands every time. This will create problems later on when you want to keep him working at the walk.

When the horse is walking well, let the reins slip through your fingers for the free walk on loose rein. This free walk is a reward for good work.

Before you go out and jump on your horse to train him to go, I want you to study the next chapter so you won't create a runaway. Remember that your horse must go forward willingly *under control*. Control must be gained in such a way that it does not destroy his willingness to go forward. Let us lay a good foundation so we cure the problems without creating new ones.

3

Controlling the Horse

Why horses run away

Horses run away because they are hurt or frightened. If the bit continually hurts the horse, he will usually just rush off with quick, choppy steps; but sudden pain can cause an out and out runaway. A horse can be frightened by an object or a noise or by confusion in his mind. The idea that the way to train a horse is just to make him do what you want can confuse him greatly. Let's suppose, for instance, that you decide to train your horse to take his leads (see Chapter 12). The left lead is fine, but he just will not take his right lead. You try and try, each time bringing him to a sudden stop because he took the wrong lead, and then goosing him into the canter to try again with the same results. Both of you end up in a lather because you think the horse is being stubborn, and he has no idea what you want because you aren't preparing him for the right lead by getting him to bend to the right. Such a battle can confuse the horse so badly that he becomes frightened and runs away.

All runaways are not hurt or frightened, however. A horse can run because your unsteady legs whammed him in the sides and told him to. He can also learn to run away because he wasn't properly and methodically trained in the beginning. Suppose a person saddles up his colt one day for the first time, just to see what he will do. He is a gentle, barnyard pet and doesn't do anything, so the person gets on and takes a turn or two around the yard. Then, because nothing bad has happened yet, he goes out for a ride, trusting to luck. Lots of times nothing bad happens since God seems to take care of these people. Too often, though, a jackrabbit jumps out from under the colt's feet or a covey of quail scutters off through the leaves nearby. The colt heads for the hills. If the rider doesn't know how to nail the colt on the first jump, a habit is born that will soon be confirmed by a similar incident.

A horse can learn to use running away quite coolly, as a means of avoiding work — although you would think that might be more work than working! The most unusual case I've come across of the disobedient runaway is Dos Reales. He is a most unusual horse with a very British sense of humor. He will pull off a joke with an absolutely straight face and it will be months before you realize it is a joke.

Dos was started by a fellow who just gets on a colt to see if he can stay on top. Dos had put him off two or three times — not by bucking but by simply making a sudden turn that landed his agile rider standing on the ground beside him. When I first rode Dos, I found out how he did it. He would run toward the fence with his body bent to turn right and at the very last moment abruptly turn left. This makes quite a surprise ending for the rider who is all set to turn right with him. But I only lost a stirrup and set Dos to thinking up a new trick or two.

Under his first rider Dos had learned that he was free to run away, which was the initial part of the reversal trick. He would run away on the longe; he would run out of the longe circle; he would run away under saddle. But he never got excited about it, except the one time I kept kicking him by accident because I lost my balance each time he almost stopped. That gave us quite a run! No, he never got excited and he always took care not to hurt his handler/rider. That is how I came to the conclusion that this was just his idea of a joke. It was just like the time I upbraided my daughter for being too rough with the kitten and she said, "I'm just helping him have fun." Dos was just helping me have fun.

The main reason that Dos kept pulling his little joke for so long was really my fault. I had just started to get involved in dressage and the dressage books say, "The horse must go forward willingly"; "Forward straight and never rein back" (Waldemar Seunig, *Horsemanship*). So in the beginning, before understanding finally dawns, we go racing around arenas, hoping that someday the horse will get tired enough that he will want to stop. During my first lesson under Mr. Friedlaender, it was quite a revelation to me when he got on my horse. He trotted Dos once around the arena and Dos thought, "Charge!" But you know, I didn't even see my horse make his move to run away because Hermann nailed him on the spot. He drove that horse right onto the bit, hard. Dos stuck his nose straight up in the air with his hind legs under him and came to a screeching halt — not a pretty one but a dead halt. Then Hermann immediately moved him on. As Hermann says, "You have to be boss." As Seunig says, "There are times when you must drop all form and simply make the horse mind."

When a person is on a horse's back, he is more or less at the horse's mercy. The more the person understands and feels horses, and the more he knows about training principles, the less he is at the mercy of the horse's whims. Lots of romantic stories have been written about the boy (or man or woman) who captures the heart of the wild stallion and so gains that horse's instant allegiance and obedience.

It is true that an occasional horse eventually gives his heart to a certain person. Dos always liked my husband better than he liked me, and the horse that Bill had before Dos liked Bill on sight. Red Cloud was hard to catch, yet he let Bill walk up to him in a large corral full of other horses. After Bill rode him and turned him loose in the corral, Red Cloud followed him to the gate. The horse I have now indicated that he belonged to me the moment I took hold of his lead rope. He was then two and a half years old and had seen me only once before when he was a yearling — pretty well ignoring me at that time. None of these horses has been completely obedient to me or to Bill.

If horses were not basically kind and forgiving, far more people would be injured and killed by them. They are strong and explosive. They are quick and accurate with their feet and teeth. But horses are basically defensive rather than offensive. That is why people can get away with just saddling up a colt and riding him without educating him; but if they don't go on to educate him properly, sooner or later most of these people write, "Dear Mary

Twelveponies, My horse won't stop . . ." (Or go or turn, etc.)

Many of these people ask me if they should use a more severe bit, and there are trainers who will recommend this kind of bit to control the horse. Then their next recommendation is a tiedown to force the horse to lower his head and accept the pain from the bit that raised his head in the first place. Some people have the notion that, since tightening the reins is part of stopping the horse, the harder you tighten them and the more severe the bit, the better the horse should stop. These people want a magical tool, a bridle of Bellerophon, to put on the horse to gain instant obedience. Putting a severe bit in a horse's mouth to control him pre-dates King Solomon, and I am sure that the highways of his day were littered with dead bodies the same way our freeways are.

As people became more and more aware of the fact that a horse could be trained instead of forced into obedience, the pendulum swung the other way. Now we have people letting their horses get away with murder because they misunderstand what is meant by light hands or by the dressage principle of "never rein back." The light hands people must learn that a light contact means leaving the contact light when the horse makes it light but otherwise being firm enough to control the horse. The dressage people shouldn't just assume that everyone has enough sense to train their horses to stop. And the proponents of the ancient art of controlling the horse with a severe bit need to learn that the pain thus inflicted can actually cause problems such as running away, bucking, and rearing.

If anyone were to tell me that his horse bucks, rears, or runs away, I would refuse to get on that horse with any type of curb bit in his mouth or harsh leverage on his nose. The first thing you have to establish with such a horse (or with any horse) is that you are bigger and stronger than he is. If you do it by inflicting pain with a leverage bit, it is just the pain that registers in his mind — not true submission to his rider as a superior herd member. That pain can actually be the cause of his disobediences. A friend told me about a colt he was starting at the track that insisted on bucking every time out. My friend finally put a rubber snaffle in the colt's mouth and he never bucked again.

With the snaffle bit you can control a horse without causing him undue pain. It isn't magic any more than any other bit is. You have to know how to use it to get control and results. I ride every colt and every horse I get on to train or retrain in a confined space to help control him until I have convinced him of my superiority. I do this by teaching him to double. Doubling (see below) is the best safety measure and training device you can know. It can be used to control any horse even if he is not trained to double.

Someone recently described to me how to throw a runaway. The person who told me this said she had done it many times; and since she stood before me still all in one piece, I could conclude that it isn't as dangerous as it sounds. However, she also said that one horse still ran off every day, even though he had been thrown time and time again. I have seen other people try to cure a horse of bolting by backing him fifty to a hundred feet — *after* stopping him by running him straight into the wall of the arena. The horse I have in mind has accumulated several miles of travel in reverse, and still he bolts. I am more interested in your safety and in curing your horses' problems than in suggesting things that might work once in a while.

Training the horse to double

Doubling is a safe and effective way to prevent and cure problems such as bolting and bucking. It isn't just turning a horse in a small circle; it is turning him "inside out" — so to speak. If you turn the horse in a small circle to control him and "to make him dizzy" as some advocate, he can rebel and run off to the outside with his head still pulled far to the inside. This is also a poor training method because the horse simply falls forward and lugs around — two things you want to discourage, not teach him.

Doubling, on the other hand, helps a horse to shift his balance toward the rear where you want it, because you turn him back on himself similarly to a turn on the haunches. It encourages rather than discourages the horse to go forward, because you move him into it and boot him out of it. It lightens his response to the snaffle, rather than teaching him to lug on it, because you release the pull the instant he will finish the turn himself. This rewards him at the appropriate time to teach him obedience. It avoids confusing him because it is over so quickly and work is immediately resumed. It is the quickest way to remind a horse that he is to keep his mind on his work, not on disobediences.

You can't double a horse with a curb bit without hurting him excessively, and I would never attempt it except in a dire emergency. Doubling should be done with a snaffle or a bosal hackamore (not a mechanical hackamore) and that is why I would never get on an outlaw with anything but a snaffle. To double a horse, slide the turning hand down the rein for a shorter hold. Then simultaneously move the other hand forward to avoid tightening *that* rein, sink your seat deep in the saddle, and firmly pull the horse's head right back toward his tail with your hand out to the side, on a level with your hips. The moment the horse is committed to the turn, release the turning rein and boot him forward. Don't turn him in a complete circle and don't let him stop. If he still wants to run away (or whatever) as you move him forward, double him back in the opposite direction and move him on.

It is very important in doubling that you release the outside contact, that you keep the horse moving forward as you double him, that you release the inside rein the moment the horse will finish the turn by himself, and that you move him forward out of the double. It is also important to remember that a high hand equals a high head, which equals poor control and improper training.

You can usually double a horse that has never been doubled before, but once in a while there is one so limber-necked or so stiff in the jaw that you will not succeed. Any horse who gives you trouble with stopping, turning, bucking, or bolting should be trained to double. I teach all of my colts to double before I ever take them out of a corral.

The best place to train a horse to double is in the round corral; but the side of a barn, a high fence, or anything else that you can trot past and turn the horse into (without his getting his head over or under it) will work. Ride the horse in a trot along your barrier (about six feet out from it); slide your hand down and

The start of doubling to the right: The rider's outside leg is back to hold the horse's haunches, the inside hand is low and pulling out to the side, to lead the horse in the direction he is to turn, while the rider looks where the horse is going to go.

Doubling to the left: At this point release the turning rein; the horse will finish the turn of his own accord. As he does, make him go forward.

turn him right into the fence. Be sure you maintain contact on the pulling (leading) rein so you don't jerk his mouth even though the pull must be abrupt and firm. Boot him around with your inside leg if he is slow to turn. From the trot he will have to stop but he should not stop turning. The moment his other eye can see the fence, release your pull because he will then finish the turn himself. Move him on and double him back the other way.

It is best to have many places where you can double a horse so he doesn't learn to expect it at any one place. When I was starting my Frosty filly, she tensed up and grabbed her tail as we trotted along one side of the arena. I doubled her, booted her out and doubled her again, and continued trotting on around. At the exact same spot she again grabbed her tail and I automatically slid my hand down to double her. That's as far as I got — she doubled herself. Horses don't often learn that quickly!

It isn't good to double a horse too much. Two to four times each way every day for a few days is usually enough to let the horse know that you can turn him any time you choose. After that you can double him outside in case of emergency against a bush too high for him to jump over or a tree with branches too low for him to duck under. You can even double a horse out in the open if necessary. But soon you can control him just by taking your hand out to the side and tightening the rein enough to turn his head slightly. It gets his attention and reminds him that you are boss.

Don't double the horse to the same side every time. This is an easy habit to fall into but it can make the horse hard to turn to the opposite side. Always keep the horse moving during doubling and as he comes out of it because you want him to continue to go forward willingly. Slowing him down too much during and after doubling gives him the mental and physical advantage he needs to pull some kind of disobedience. Doubling gets your horse's attention — take advantage of it by going on with the work at hand.

Doubling is not only a safety device, it is also a good training tool to get a horse to turn easily and to balance himself back toward the rear. As a training device, though, I use it first in the walk and gradually build up to more speed. I have trained the horse to double for safety's sake but want him to develop his agility according to his physical ability. Today doubling is much over-used by western trainers. I got a letter from one girl who had bought a trained horse and every time she cantered him near an arena fence, he would double himself back. Through rote the horse had been taught the words but not their meaning. A technique that can be a good training tool if used wisely had been misused and had developed a problem in the horse. There are no problem horses . . .

There are some basic principles you need to know about teaching a horse to turn before I get into curing bad habits. The first one is that a horse will not turn well if he is not going forward willingly. So when your horse is sluggish in turning, always remember to drive him more with your legs and whip rather than using the reins more.

When a horse stiffens his jaw and refuses to yield to your inside rein when you ask him to turn, it is true that if you do not pull, he will not pull — but he will not turn either. Doubling is the first step in educating the horse that insists on "bulling" on the rein like this. Don't try to double him while he is bulling. First quit asking for the turn; next boot him forward and then double him to that side and boot him out. If you try to double him without releasing him first, he will just lug around in a little

A walking turn to the left. You automatically teach the horse to neckrein if you turn in the waist to look where you are going.

A walking turn to the right. The fence helps the horse to shift his balance to the rear and finish the turn on a loose rein.

circle, which does no good. You want him moving, not leaning on the rein.

Turning with the leading rein

The next step in turning is using the leading rein, which can be used instead of doubling if the horse is not bulling badly. In doubling you take your hand out to the side about even with your hips. This is the leading rein; but in using it as a leading rein, you just take enough to turn the horse's head slightly and then release it. If you get this leading rein by rotating your forearm out from the elbow so your fingernails are on top (knuckles down) you automatically maintain contact; you control the amount of pull by the distance you turn your forearm out; and you release it by moving your forearm back toward normal position. This gives you very tactful control of the leading rein so you can take as much as you need to, immediately start the release, and be in position to take again or finish the release as needed. Use it as a brief reminder to the horse, not as a steady aid all through the turn. It is very valuable because it doesn't slow the horse down and it doesn't bend his neck when it is done properly.

The leading rein

Trained to double and respond to the leading rein, Iam starts turning when he sees my hand move out.

Always use your leg aids (inside leg driving on the girth and outside leg back a little to hold the haunches) and turn in the waist to look in the direction of the turn. Never try to force a horse through a turn by pulling straight back on the rein. You will just bend his neck that way and his body can go where it pleases. Never try to force a horse to turn by neckreining him either (see p. 134). Always use a leading rein to help a horse turn when he is disobedient to neckreining. When he is thoroughly trained, you can correct his resistance to it by swatting, kicking, or spurring him to move him, but never by applying stronger pressure to his neck. That just bends his neck and tilts his head.

The basics of controlling a horse are moving him forward and doubling him. Now we can get on with explaining how to train the horse in turning and stopping, and how to handle him in specific problems.

PART II
Problems
Under Saddle

*But they obeyed not,
neither inclined their ear,
but made their neck stiff,
that they might not hear,
nor receive instruction.*
— JEREMIAH 17:23

Iam stops as I apply the
aids properly.

4

The Barnsour Horse

Causes of barnsourness

It is instinctive for a horse to want to stay on his home range. This love for home plus his almost infallible sense of direction makes the horse reliable in taking you home. Knowing this can help you out if you are lost and can help you understand why so many horses are reluctant to leave home and so anxious to get back there; but it doesn't solve your problems in getting them to go where you want, at the speed you want. Judging from my mail for the last ten years, the barnsour horse is the main problem people have. The solution is simple — make the horse obedient and you will have no trouble. The trouble is how to do this.

One girl with a balky horse wrote, "Please help quickly because if I switch her I know it hurts terribly bad and I don't want to hurt her at all." This sort of misplaced sympathy is terribly bad for the horse's training. If a horse needs a swat, he will accept it almost gladly. Unjust punishment (such as a series of swats that mean nothing to him except that he is being hurt) makes him fearful and often resentful. A single swat with the whip means "move at attention" and should be used for that purpose when needed. Your horse will respect you for that.

Another area of misguided sympathy is in the handling of the reins. If you ride with a loose rein so you won't hurt the horse's mouth, you are bound to jerk on it when you suddenly discover he isn't going where you intended. Here you are worrying about how much the whip would hurt him, and you end up suddenly jerking on his mouth in an effort to keep him going in the desired direction. To the horse that is punishment for moving, so he gets discouraged and decides going forward is for the dummies. You must ride with contact on all disobedient horses and must carry a whip on most of them.

The biggest reason you cannot make a barnsour horse leave or stay away from home without a big fuss is that he knows you cannot control him. Another problem may be that the horse knows that most of the ride will be torture. The torture can come from ill-fitting or dirty equipment, poor grooming under the equipment, or a rider that sits off-balance. All of these things can cause sore spots. The torture can also come from being ridden hard over poor footing and jerked to a fast stop or turn. Even if none of these things happen, the ride can be torture to the horse if he has to carry a poor rider who pounds his back and jerks his mouth with every stride. Going out for a ride may not be what the horse planned for the day's activities, but he ought to be comfortable while he has to do it.

The first thing to do with a barnsour horse is to check him over for sore places in his mouth, under his chin, at his poll, on his back, and under the cinch. Use finger pressure on his back and sides because they can be sore even though no abrasions are evident. Fix or replace any ill-fitting equipment. Get a regular snaffle bit with a thick mouthpiece and ring cheeks, and get reins that fit your hands. Get a riding whip or cut a willowy stick.

Teaching the horse to be obedient

Do not try to leave home on a barnsour horse until you have retrained him to be quite obedient. Do not think for a minute that riding him only at home will make him more stubborn about leaving and more anxious to get back. It is the control you establish by schooling him at home that wins the battles and prevents the war. You can start retraining the horse in an area as small as a 50-foot corral but should eventually branch out to an area as large as 60' by 100' — whatever area you have at home that's at least partially confined by buildings, fences, brush, or trees.

The first thing to do is to train your horse to go forward willingly and to double (see Chapters 2 and 3). Both of these will

Sitting off-balance is one of the things that can make a horse uncomfortable and reluctant to be ridden.

give you better control of your horse since he must slow down to pull most of his disobediences and doubling convinces him that you can prevent his running away. Soon he will give up his idea of bolting forward as soon as you take one hand out to the side and tighten the rein enough to turn his head slightly. From that you can train him to stop reliably.

Training the horse to stop

When you ask a horse to stop, you must let your weight down into the saddle, close your legs on his sides, and brace your elbows against your sides. If you then inhale deeply, the horse will stop. If you lean forward, push down with your feet, and bring your arms back, all you are doing is pulling on the horse's mouth, and that just supports him so he can keep going. If you pull up your knees and heels when you try to close your legs on his sides, that takes your weight off his back and nullifies your stopping aids. Check your riding habits.

It is easy to tell you how to ask a horse to stop so he really will stop on command, but you are not going to change your way of riding overnight. In the meantime, you have this Mr. Hyde that you're trying to change back to Dr. Jekyll, so I will tell you a

Loose reins let a disobedient horse pull his tricks, and make you jerk his mouth when you try to regain control.

couple of things that can help you train him to stop on command. After you have taught the horse to double, ride him in a walk close alongside your barrier. To ask him to halt, take your outside hand (on the same side as the barrier) out to the side about a foot and say "Ho" as you apply the aids for stopping. The horse will start to turn his head and will stop because he sees the barrier in his way. Try to apply all the stopping aids correctly as you do this and relax the aids the moment he stops. Pet him; ride him on and come back around to do it again.

Leaning forward and pulling on the reins lets the horse keep right on going.

By doing this two or three times in each direction, you will start to get him in the habit of stopping on command. Then you can ask him this same way at other places, first where there is a bush or fence to turn his head toward and then out in the open. When he is getting consistent about stopping on command, you can tighten one rein or the other without taking your hand out to the side and without turning his head.

Another method is to walk the horse straight toward a barrier, using two leading reins on contact to keep him from turning to either side. When he is almost up to the barrier, give him the stopping aids without letting him turn either way. The barrier will stop him so you don't need to make the mistake of pulling back on the reins. Pet him to show him he did what you wanted. When you go on after this to stopping without a barrier, be sure to have plenty of open space ahead of the horse. If he is near the barrier, he will want to walk up to it before stopping.

Encouraging the horse to yield to the bit

Because you are probably in the habit of pulling on the reins (90 percent of us are), your horse no doubt sticks his nose out and stiffens his jaw when you ask him to stop. After you have made two or three training stops, start asking the horse to yield to the bit before moving him on. Do this by taking equal contact on the reins with his head straight. Then set one hand by clamping your elbow to your side. If you have noticed that your horse turns more easily to one side than the other, that is the side on which you should fix your hand. Then roll the other hand in and out in a slow rhythm, bending your wrist to do this. This flexes his head to the side, making him come against the contact on the fixed rein. This will relax the tension in his neck and jaw and cause him to tuck his nose — and yield to the bit. The moment he tucks his nose down and back, relax both hands without moving them forward. Do this as you ride him forward, too, fixing your outside hand and rolling your inside one. When the horse yields by tucking his nose, be sure that *you relax your hands.* When the

Ride on contact and encourage the horse to yield to the bit while moving forward energetically. Here Iam is still resisting.

The horse that overbends this way can do pretty much as he pleases. Drive him forward without pulling on the reins.

horse yields to the bit, the contact gets light and you want to leave it that way. *Warning:* do not try to force or pull his nose back so his face is in the vertical. This can cause him to overbend at the poll or even to go *behind* the bit (drop contact), which is a worse problem than his boring into the bit. All you want him to do now is relax his jaw so the contact is light and so he will respond to the bit without resistance. If he does overbend (see photo), drive him forward without pulling on the reins.

In asking for the halt, tighten one rein slightly more than the other — but not always the same one — to remind the horse of the doubling. When he comes to a halt, exhale so you relax your aids. This will keep him from feeling that he is in a bind and needs to get out of it by moving around. It also rewards him for his obedience. Asking a horse to change from the canter to the trot or walk and from the trot to the walk is just the same as asking him to stop. The difference is that you relax the stopping aids as he is making the change (transition) so you can push him on in the new gait. Your initial obedience work should be done mostly in the trot with some walk in between because this gives you the best chance to control the horse.

In this retraining at home you want to make your horse thoroughly obedient, so see to it that he does each thing you ask and does not do anything you do not ask. He should walk and trot and turn and stop *when and where you tell him to,* not when and where he decides he wants to. Be firm and consistent but not routine. If you do each thing at the same place every time, you will only teach him a pattern, not obedience. Work in the walk and trot to get your horse to go forward with energy, turn easily, take the trot, and come back to the walk without hesitation. Work on his halts toward the end of each lesson when he is not so eager to keep going. That way you don't risk his walking on through your stop aids. While it is essential to good training to make the horse do each thing you ask, it is also wise to ask only what you can enforce at the moment.

Check out your way of riding. Be sure you sit squarely in the middle, that you stay relaxed in the waist and keep your legs stretched down without pushing on the stirrups so you won't pound his back. Stay relaxed in your shoulders and elbows so your hands won't constantly jerk his mouth. If you have trouble riding the trot, you can take the forward position and keep your hands on the horse's neck during all riding until your balance and relaxation improve. You can't be jerking the horse's mouth when you ride — especially not every time you ask him to move forward, because that just tells him you don't really want him to go.

You must ride with a definite contact with the horse's mouth so you have instant control of him. You must stay alert to keep him going at the speed you want, in the gait you want, and in the direction you want. I was doing a neighbor's chores for him for a few days and those chores included feeding the chickens. In the pen with them was a huge red rooster that had been taught to fight. For three days I kept my mind on that rooster even when my back was turned while I put out the feed and water. On the last day as I was almost finished in the chicken pen, I let my mind wander to self-congratulations that the rooster had not spurred me once. That is when he hit me!

Concentrate on your work. If you go to sleep and let your horse have his own way once in a while during this retraining period, he will think there will always be a chance that he can hit you with a disobedience in an off moment. Use firm enough aids that you get obedience, but don't expect your horse to be perfect in the beginning. Praise him often for a little bit of good work, then more good work will follow.

Horses have several ways of refusing to go where you want them to go. Some just plain stop; but unless the horse is a true balker, he usually follows this with whirling toward the barn or corral as soon as he feels he is in full control. He may stop and rear, buck, or run sideways or backward. A few horses will try to rub the rider off on trees, barns, or fences.

When he is being ridden at home, your horse may not try his favorite getting-his-own-way tricks. Don't let this fool you into thinking he is truly obedient. If you can't control him away from home, you are not really controlling him at home. Make him start working with energy. Each time you feel him start to lose energy, drive him on and then control his speed tactfully in the next few strides. At the beginning of each lesson, it is okay to ride him around and around to establish energy, rhythm, and relaxation; but once these are established, start picking out points ahead to make a change of gait, a turn, a circle, or a halt. This way you are definite in your mind what you want your horse to do and will be more definite in asking him to do it. After five or ten minutes of work, at a moment when he is working well, reward him with a minute of walk on loose rein. Then pick up the reins and work him some more.

You must always be prepared to hit the horse that stops suddenly of his own accord, preferably just as he thinks of stopping instead of after he has stopped. Hit him with the whip hard enough that he keeps moving. Some horses will buck or kick out when hit like this, so be ready to hit him again to punish him for bucking or kicking.

When I was starting Pi Dough under saddle, I found he could stop the quickest with the least warning of any horse I had ridden. Most colts can simply be booted into moving forward, but not Pi Dough; so I took down my quirt and headed him in a brisk trot away from the barn. Paying strict attention to him, I was able to swat him hard just as he started to stop. Immediately two things happened at once. He bogged his head to buck. I brought my hand forward to take hold of the rein. This made the quirt swing around and catch him squarely on the nose. Up went his head and onward he trotted. Now I never recommend hitting a horse anywhere on the head, and this was quite an accident; but the timing was perfect so I convinced him not only that he must not stop unasked but must not buck either.

A whip is easier to control than a quirt because it is stiffer and you don't have to let go of the rein in order to hit the horse. It is easier with the whip to hit the horse at the exact right time. Don't be afraid to hit hard enough the first time or two to convince the horse you mean business. If your horse bucks or kicks out for being hit, keep your contact with his mouth so he can't bog his head as you hit him again. Keeping him moving briskly will prevent further bucking and kicking.

If your horse is stubborn about turning, even going off in the opposite direction, take a look at his neck as you try to turn him. You will find that it is well bent just in front of the withers. A horse with such a limber neck is very hard to control. To cure it teach him two things — to double and to go forward on equal contact. In doubling remember that you must drop the outside contact and use the fence to help turn the horse. Even though you pull the horse's head around to start the double, it will not make him more limber-necked because the fence makes him sit back; and releasing the pull when he will finish the turn himself lets him straighten his neck. Double your horse just enough each way to be able to do it easily, showing yourself that you have convinced your horse you can turn him.

In teaching the horse to go forward on equal contact, ride with your hands a foot or more apart so you "frame" him between the

The limber-necked horse can run out sideways to avoid turning and even rub you against fences and trees.

reins. Keep him moving forward well in the walk and make wide turns with a leading rein. If you keep the outside contact and use the leading rein to lead him through the turn, you should be able to get wide turns without bending his neck. If he doesn't turn or if he goes sideways in the opposite direction, don't pull on the turning rein whatever you do because this will just bend his neck. Instead, use the whip to keep him going forward, and be satisfied with getting him turned somewhere in the direction you ask. This kind of horse takes lots of patient work and every time you bend his neck in an effort to enforce the turn, you are slowing your progress. Do not pull. Use your legs and whip to move him and make him turn.

In all turns, look where you want to go by turning in the waist and letting your hands move with your body. If you pull back on the outside rein, the horse cannot turn. If you drop contact on the outside rein, he can bend his neck. When he has made two or three good, wide turns in each direction in the walk, trot him on and make several turns, still keeping your hands about a foot apart, going straight and using the leading rein for turning. Change your leg aids as you approach the turn so the horse will know the turn is coming. By thoroughly retraining your horse

"Framing" the horse between two leading reins on contact can help you keep him going straight ahead.

this way, you can gradually stop using the leading rein and stop holding your hands farther apart. Just remember — to make a horse turn you must drive him forward, not pull him back.

One of my students had the most limber-necked horse I have ever seen. When I tried to turn this horse, he ran off to the outside. When I tried to trot him straight forward, he went off at an angle; and when I swatted him with the whip, he came to a crushing halt sideways into the wall of the arena. I immediately pushed him away from the wall with my hand — even a small person on a fair-sized horse can do this — and hit him once as hard as I could on that side. He moved on! Using the method I have just described, I got him turning, circling, and trotting down the track. Just once he thought about crowding me into the wall again. As I felt him veer toward the wall, I zinged him with the whip on that side. That convinced him. You have to be the boss; do not hesitate to prove it.

Retraining a horse takes lots of patience and a certain amount of cold-blooded correction. Punish your horse when he needs it in the amount that he needs. If you wait until his disobediences have made you mad, you will overpunish him and it will probably be at the wrong time. Right now when he is starting the disobedience is the right time. Ask your horse to work. If you don't, he will think he never has to work. Making him work hard at home not only teaches him obedience — it has the added benefit of making him more anxious to leave home for a relaxing pleasure ride.

5

Refusal to Go

Curing specific ways of resisting

If you stay alert to keep your horse moving whenever he thinks about dragging along instead of after it is an accomplished fact, you will get him over the notion that he can stop whenever he pleases. That takes care of the horse that simply stops when you and he have any conflict of interests. It also takes care of a horse that bucks or kicks out, but some of the other tricks of his trade require doubling in combination with driving the horse forward. Before you consider taking your horse away from home again, both driving him forward and doubling him should become reflex actions for you.

While these two things are general preventives and cures of most problems, you need to know how to apply them specifically. I have told you how to retrain the limber-necked horse that runs out to the side instead of turning (p. 47). This takes lots of hours of consistent work on a badly spoiled horse and is quite necessary if you want to be able to control your horse under all circumstances. In the meantime emergencies may crop up. If your horse still bends his neck and runs out (in spite of your two leading reins and driving him forward), tap him on that outside shoulder with the whip. He is leading with that shoulder when he runs out in that direction. Hitting him on it will make him think he has run into something, thus making him pull the shoulder back in line so he can go on and turn.

If he does not respond to being hit on the outside shoulder, briefly stop trying to turn him. Boot him ahead and double him. For instance, if you are asking him to turn right and he is running out to the left, boot him straight ahead and double him to the left. Doubling to the left instead of the right keeps him from lugging around. Boot him out; double him back to the right and ride him on through the right turn with two leading reins. Don't give him time to think. Keep him moving and make the turn while you still have his attention.

This same doubling treatment applies to the horse that suddenly whirls around. If at all possible, double him right on around so his spin is 360°. If you can't catch him quick enough for that and he has started off in the opposite direction, double him back the other way, frame him with two leading reins (see p. 47) and move him forward. Whenever you double a horse to get him going in the desired direction, stop turning him and start driving him straight ahead *before* you have him pointed where you want him to go. If you try to get him pointed right first and then release the pull and start driving, he will be able to turn on around to the direction he wants to go.

A horse that tries to rub his rider off on trees or fences is being hurt in the mouth or is confused by what you ask of him or by the way you ask it. If this is your problem, you definitely need the instruction on seat and aids in *Everyday Training: Backyard Dressage* and lots of practice in using that instruction. When your horse tries to give you the brush-off, remember to use your whip on the side of the trees, fence, or barn instead of on the side away from them. Doing that would just drive him closer to them.

The horse that follows his refusal to go with rearing, jumping up and down, or running backward is usually being held too hard with the reins at the same time he is being told to go forward. If he does these things on a loose rein, he probably learned them from being held too tightly in the first place. The first thing to remember is that you can't stop a horse from doing these things by pulling on the reins. Since you tighten the reins to ask a horse to stop, it seems to be reflex action for a lot of people to tighten them to ask a horse to stop jumping up and down or going backward.

Don't even think about getting the horse to stop what he is doing. Instead think only of making him move forward. Don't lean forward yourself because that lightens your seat and frees the horse for his own devices. Lean back to press your seat deeper into the saddle, give the horse a slightly loose rein, and swat him with the whip. Get him moving and then take the contact again without jerking on his mouth. At the same time *keep him moving*. While this definitely works on all three of these problems, it can be dangerous on two of them — rearing and jumping up and down. I consider rearing such a dangerous problem that I will go into detail on it separately. The danger with the "jumping" horse is that he might run away, so be prepared to double him if you feel him bunch himself to bolt. Proper doubling will control him and keep him moving.

One person wrote that the first time he tried to ride his colt, it would only move backward. Figuring that this was at least moving even if in the wrong direction, this person encouraged it, only to find the colt using it against him whenever he did not want to go forward. When a horse has discovered how helpless his rider is to control him when he is moving backward, he will most likely just go back faster when hit with the whip no matter how loose the reins are. I would double this horse half a turn and swat him hard as I released the pull, repeating this procedure until I got him moving forward. Then I would tell him what a good boy he is and encourage him to keep moving each time I felt him start to slow down. I would prefer to work him in the trot to make it easier to keep him going forward. He also needs lots of praise when he is going forward.

One time I saw a little different case of a horse going backward instead of forward. When she got started back, she would back rapidly until she lost her footing and sat down — all this no matter how loose the reins were. This mare was very well reined and so obedient that, when her green rider went to bridle her by simply standing in front of her and holding up the bridle, she closed her eyes in anticipation of pain, opened her mouth and took the bit. Checking out the equipment, I found that the curb strap was so tight there was no relief from it at any time. All it took to cure this problem was to adjust the curb strap properly.

Barnsour horses usually have their favorite spots for balking. Any time a horse gets away with a disobedience, you should be prepared for him to pull that same one again at that same spot or even some other place. If you react immediately when you feel the horse preparing to do it again, you can nip a bad habit in the bud and save yourself a lot of work. Experienced trainers know most of the defenses horses use to get out of work and so they stay alert all through the basic training to prevent the horse's getting away with them the first time. The more obedient you make your horse, the fewer things he will try in order to get his own way.

When your horse is already badly spoiled, you have to stay doubly alert to prevent his getting away with his favorite disobedience. Since he is in the habit of disobeying, you may find him adopting other methods when his favorite one no longer works. That means you have to know how to handle all these things I have told you about — not just the one or two that your horse usually does. Keep in mind that you are going to spend several weeks or even months retraining your horse, that it will be work, but it will pay off in the end by making your horse reliable for whatever you want him to do.

Gaining the horse's trust

Gain your horse's trust (as well as his obedience) by praising him for good work, riding him so he is comfortable under you, and helping him regain the joy of moving forward. Asking a horse to take rough trails and make fast stops and quick turns before he is

Get your horse to go forward willingly and to relax like this before you even consider taking him away from home again.

With mutual trust, respect, and a little patience you can "talk" your horse into any reasonable thing.

physically and mentally ready will destroy his trust in you. He will be sure to mistrust you if you blame him for doing it wrong when you are the one who did not clearly tell him what you want him to do. Mutual pleasure in riding comes with your being the benevolent boss.

How to start riding out again

When you feel that you have gained control of your horse by making him thoroughly obedient to go, turn, and stop at home, it is time to start riding out again. Remember that you are not just going out for a pleasure ride — you are going out to complete your horse's training. The first thing to do is to plan your route. If you just go out somewhere, your horse will sense your indecision and be prepared to try to direct traffic himself. If you know exactly where you are going to go, you will be more determined to make your horse go there. Plan to go to one or two places where he might act up so you can show him that you are in control.

The methods of prevention and control I have described for the various forms of disobedience apply at home and abroad. Your best defense is a good offense, which is simply to keep your horse moving forward with energy. If he never pulled any of his funnies at home, don't think he won't try out where he always tried them. Don't let anxiety spoil your ride, but have it thoroughly in your mind what to do for each thing he may try. Be relaxed, alert, and decisive in each thing you ask of your horse. Many short rides on a variety of routes will do more good right now than one or two long ones because this lessens the chance of your letting your mind wander. Look ahead to where you want to go and go there.

There are lots of subtle variations of these balky problems — all of them disobediences. For instance, there is the horse that lays his ears back when told to go forward better or to change to the trot or canter from the walk. He is just saying that he is the boss horse. Flip him with the whip for it. That says you are the boss. Horses that kick out when they are hit or kicked by their riders also want to be boss; although when you hit or kick harder than necessary to get the change of gait, you can cause such a reaction (see p. 103). Experiment to see how much you need to use your aids to get the change to the trot or canter; but if the horse bucks or kicks, regardless of the reason, do as I told you — immediately hit the horse again for kicking or bucking. This is more than punishment; it tells him to move. Remember, a horse cannot kick or buck if he is going forward with energy.

Some people have written to me saying that their horses will go just so far from home before they stop. The only way these

This horse is resisting his rider and not going forward willingly. Loose reins won't help a horse go forward better. Pick up a contact and use your legs to get the rear in gear.

Hitting a horse too hard
can make him kick out
like this. Start easy and
get progressively firmer if
you find that it's needed.
(Photo by Mark Thiffault)

riders can get their horses to move in the direction they want to
go is to get off and lead them. These horses are well aware that
they are getting their riders off their backs. After doing your
homework in the ring, ride your horse out to his favorite stopping place. If you still cannot make him move on, turn him back
toward home, boot him into a trot and immediately double him.
Boot him out in the desired direction and keep him moving.
Repeat this — doubling first to one side and then the other —
until he does go on. Do *not* get off and lead him. That makes him
the winner.

Horses and ponies that stop suddenly to eat grass are just disrespectful. I hate to ride a colt with anyone who lets his horse do
this. The colt immediately wants to do the same and that makes
me have to hit him more than I like. Too often I am behind that
horse and my colt has nowhere to go when I hit him to make
him move and bring his head up. I never let my horse graze
when I am mounted or when he is bridled. If I want to graze him
during a rest stop, I dismount and remove the bridle so he learns
when he is allowed to eat and when he is not.

Ponies are especially good at these pauses for refreshments —
partly because kids don't keep their minds on riding and partly
because they aren't strong enough to keep the ponies' heads up.
It is of no use to try to pull the head up once the animal has it
down. While you can help keep the horse from putting his head
down by clamping your hands on the reins and bracing your

hands against the saddle, the only way to prevent and cure this annoying habit is to hit the horse hard on his body or rump just as he thinks of putting his head down. If he has already got it down, hit him hard and repeatedly to get him to move on energetically. Moving on is what makes him bring his head up and keep it up. If you can time it to hit him every time just as he thinks of putting his head down to grab a bite, you can cure him of trying — but only if you never let him graze when you are mounted.

The horse that is herdbound is disobedient in just the same way as the barnsour horse. He may leave home with you okay and give no trouble out on the trail, but he doesn't want to leave any horse or horses that you are riding with. The horse that gives you a lot of static over leaving his buddies isn't really obedient when going with the gang — just amenable. He goes along very nicely doing whatever the other horses do; and because of this, you don't realize that you are actually just a passenger. Then comes the parting of the ways and the dawning of truth — your horse thinks he is boss.

Rental horses that are taken over the same trails day in and day out with a guide in the lead learn to take a certain place in line and stay on the trail no matter what their riders do. That is what you are teaching your horse when you simply let him tag along instead of telling him where you want him to go. To retrain this horse to go where you want, start paying more attention during all of your riding. Whether you are riding alone or with others, don't put him on automatic pilot to follow the trail. Turn off to go around trees or brush along the way or to take an alternate route. When riding with others, gradually make these side trips longer and farther away until you can get out of their sight and come back without trouble. Insist that your horse go forward with energy so you keep his attention on you and keep him from slowing down to act up.

Some horses won't go out on the trail without another horse, and a few won't go out with any other horses. Neither type ever goes forward willingly on command and both need the home-study course in that basic necessity before being ridden out. For those few riders who have the seemingly exclusive type of horse, remember that horses instinctively start establishing a pecking order when they are together. A horse that won't go out with other horses is usually the more timid type that would naturally be lower in the social order.

After schooling this horse at home to get him more obedient about going forward, ride with a friend whose horse is obedient and not too pushy. Ride behind the other horse to start with — far enough back (at least a horse's length behind) that you can see his heels between your horse's ears so your horse will not feel threatened. Ride your horse actively to keep his attention; don't just let him follow along. When your horse relaxes, you can ride side-by-side and in the lead for short periods. Your friend should be a rider who is aware of his horse's body language so he can firmly close his legs on his horse to correct any intimidating moves his horse might make, such as swishing his tail or swinging his head at your horse.

Horses react differently when they are first ridden with others. A while ago I attended a riding clinic with an Arabian gelding I was training. It was his first time with more than one other horse and his reaction on entering the ring was, "Whoop-de-do! Let's have fun!" I had to ride him in an adjoining ring until I could keep his attention enough to control him. Even then when we went back in with the group he would slow down when a horse came up behind him and speed up when a horse was in front of him. Being a brave little fellow, he just wanted to socialize.

On the other hand my horse, Iam, is naively friendly but still low in the pecking order. I was riding him in a small, covered arena where I had ridden him alone several times; but this time we were with three other horses. I soon found his attention slipping and felt him getting rather nervous. Assessing the situation, I realized that he felt threatened by the others and trapped in this enclosed area; so I stopped him in the center and dismounted to talk to him and reassure him. Both of these horses were basically obedient, but each one reacted according to his own personality. I, too, reacted according to each personality and both of them soon learned to go nicely in a group.

While basic obedience is of prime importance, it is also important to consider your horse's temperament so you can handle each situation sympathetically as well as firmly. If you push a horse into panic or try to demand obedience in a situation where you cannot maintain his attention, you will end up the loser. Until your horse is thoroughly trained, every ride will present some training situation. Demand obedience but with understanding and tact. Occasionally the best offense is a discreet retreat — momentarily.

Horses that will not go in the lead are the more timid ones. The lead horse always feels a responsibility to watch for danger, and the timid horse does not care to accept this responsibility. It takes sympathetic urging to move this horse forward in the lead. While he will walk out better behind other horses, you should give him some experience being the leader, preferably in short doses each time. Natural leaders will move out better when in front but either go to sleep or keep making a bid to get ahead when they are in the rear. If you have two natural leaders, the one in front will want to move from side to side in an effort to keep the other horse from getting beside and then ahead of him.

All riders in a group should stay alert to prevent these subtle, instinctive moves and make their horses go straight forward in whatever position the riders choose. Don't let your horse drift sideways into another horse beside you or swing his head in that horse's direction. If you feel him swish his tail at the horse behind you, close your legs firmly to squelch this threat to kick. Change your respective positions often to make all horses more obedient and versatile in group riding. Horses can learn good social manners by human standards if their human masters make an understanding effort to teach them.

True balking

Dear Mary Twelveponies,

I have been riding in gymkhanas and my three-year-old filly is good at it, but now I have this weird problem with her. When I get her in the arena, she just stands by the fence and won't move. I have tried being patient and talking to her, spurring her and whipping her. None of these work. The minute she gets in that arena, she just won't budge. I love the shows, but I also love my horse. How can I get her to love them as much as I do?

Entering an improperly schooled horse in games can cause confusion that may lead to balking or rearing.

This filly is a true balker and the letter tells us how she got that way. She is barely old enough to be ridden an hour a day in simple walk, trot, and canter with wide turns and easy stops. She could be ridden as long as two hours a day on trails on rolling hills. Yet her owner is using her in games that require great athletic ability in speed and handiness. Starting with a four-year-old, it requires two years of basic and specific training for a horse to learn gymkhana work without suffering physical, mental, and emotional damage. Some horses become balkers when asked to work beyond their physical development and/or level of understanding. Others become hyperactive.

This filly became confused and discouraged and now refuses to budge. Older horses can become balkers, too, for the same reasons; and it is fairly common among rental horses that are just turned loose with the public. True balkers all display the same general style — whether they have been asked to do the one job that has finally gotten them down or just any time during work of any kind: They simply come to a grinding halt and refuse to take another step. The more you try to make them move, the more glued to the ground they become.

There is only one way to use a balker effectively. That is to stop him before he decides to stop. When my husband worked on a

This well-trained pony ran every speed event without excitement or error.

ranch, he was given such horses to drive because he could sense when they were about to stop and freeze up. He would stop them first, give them wisps of new-mown hay to eat, readjust the harness, and then go on with the work when they were relaxed. Over a period of time you can cure balkers by consistently handling them this way, but even then a rough handler could make them revert to balking.

One time when I was working at a rental stable, the owner asked me to get on one of the rental horses that would refuse to leave the barn. After I was mounted, he said, "Hang on! I'm going to get behind him with the blacksnake and teach him a lesson." I emphatically told him not to do that. I rode the horse toward the exit and stopped him before he reached it. It took him only about half a minute to relax so I could move him on out of the barn. Although this kind of handling would cure the horse if used consistently by fair or better riders, there is no way to cure such a rental horse permanently — even with a bullwhip — because he usually must continue to go out to do uncomfortable work under poor riders.

A balker requires a very sensitive rider who can feel the horse getting ready to come to a stop. When you feel that, you stop the horse and dismount as if that is your reason for stopping. Carry on a matter-of-fact conversation with him. Pick grass and feed it to him, or feed him carrots that you have brought along for that purpose. Rub him in places that might itch and readjust the tack.

At scary obstacles use
sympathetic firmness
rather than brute force.
Avoid developing balking.

You must be very relaxed yourself, very patient, and very aware
to know when the horse has relaxed so he will be willing to
move on. It isn't stubbornness that makes him balk — it is mental and emotional trauma caused by his unhappy experiences. It
is a temporary nervous breakdown.

You would think that stopping and getting off would be a
reward for balking, but remember that you are the one that
stopped the horse so you are rewarding him for obedience. This is
a very good example of how important the timing of reward and
punishment is to a horse. If you petted him to relax him *after* he
balked, he would certainly feel rewarded for balking. That brief
second needed for you to stop him first makes it possible to
reward him and get good results. Once he has balked, there is
nothing you can do because no punishment will move him or
prevent future balking. His mind is just as frozen as his body is at
that point.

The balker can be rehabilitated by starting his training all over
again and patiently taking him step-by-step along the education
trail. You must use only positive reward, never punishment. If he
balks at anything in the training, you must figure out how to
explain what you want without triggering his trauma. You have
to be a person with great sympathetic understanding of horses, a
person who knows how to get a horse to trust you. You can get a
lot of work out of a balker if you remember that he is a slower
thinker who will simply freeze up when faced with a dilemma or

with the kind of situation that started his balking in the first place.

Horses that balk at one specific problem (such as the young filly at gymkhanas) aren't as difficult to rehabilitate. This filly just needs to be put through thorough basic obedience training with no gymkhana work. Make sure you take her step-by-step according to her stage of development and level of understanding. Make sure you don't give her contradictory commands such as jerking on her mouth as you ask her to speed up.

Once she is thoroughly retrained and properly ridden, she could again be schooled and used in gymkhanas. Before she is actually ridden in such events, she should be taken to several of them to be ridden around in the arena just to get her relaxed. Then she should be ridden through several events just for relaxed experience, not for speed. She certainly isn't going to like those games if the experience is painful and confusing for her.

Curing variations on balking

Some colts refuse to move when first mounted. If the colt will not move when you tap him with the whip, you can usually get him moving by pulling his head to one side or the other to get him off-balance enough that he has to take a step. Then if you are quick enough to release the pull as he takes the step, you can manage to keep him going with light taps with the whip. But some colts will not move no matter what you do, and hitting them hard would just invite them to buck.

These colts feel that they cannot carry their riders — at least not in balance. They are not stubborn or balky, just unsure. If such a colt will move when he is led with a rider on him, he should be led around for a while. At first the rider should squeeze with his legs as the person on the ground tells the colt to walk on. Next the rider can get the colt to move first with the leading person just reinforcing it if necessary. Gradually the person leading the colt can get more and more out of the picture, doing so while the colt is in motion.

A colt that starts balking after being ridden several times is becoming a true balker. He may be too young and/or inexperienced for the type and amount of work he is being asked to do. The rider may be jerking his mouth and pounding his back. Any time a horse plants his feet and refuses to move from a sudden, hard swat with the whip, stop all activity and take stock of the way you ride, what you are asking of your horse, and what condition your horse is in. It is no fun at all trying to use a true balker, and it is a shame if you are the one who made him that way.

Turning the colt's head just enough to get him off-balance can help get him moving again.

6

Runaways

Besides refusing to leave home, the barnsour horse may want to run for home every time he is headed in that direction. If he gets away with it, he is a runaway. If he prances, he is an abomination. Horses may run away for other reasons, such as Dos Reales with his sense of humor. Some horses invent boogers. Others are actually scared or hurt. Whatever the excuse, a horse runs away because he can get away with it, and he prances because some rider along the way either thought it a fancy parade gait that shows spirit or just did not know how to prevent it.

The runaway should be trained at home and the means of controlling him is doubling (see Chapter 3). It is also important to train him to go forward willingly, which may seem odd to you, but willingness to go forward and rushing off excitedly are two different things. The excited horse is just that — excited and often wishing he could escape a rough rider and harsh bit. If the excitement and pain overpower him, he will try to escape by running, bucking, or rearing. The horse that calculates to run away will slow down first, waiting for that moment when he can take his rider by surprise. Therefore, if you can make your horse relax and go forward willingly, you can thwart his getting the advantage to bolt and run.

The steps in training a horse to stop reliably are the same whether the horse is spoiled or just green. It is just much easier if he has never found out he can run away. You start with training him to double, so you have control and so he responds to the tightening of one rein. If you pull on both reins equally, the horse can use the bit to support himself so he can go that much faster. Doubling him into a wall of some sort helps turn him and also gives him the notion that you have control and can stop him — even though you keep him moving out during doubling.

When your horse has accepted doubling, he will remember that you are in control whenever he sees your hand go out to the side and feels that one rein tighten. Then that is all you usually need to control his initial bolt for freedom, and you can simply keep him moving on with controlled energy. It is important in controlling a horse by doubling or by taking one rein out to the side, that you do it in that first leap forward, or sooner when you feel him think about running. After he is fully running, you can easily throw him down in doubling him and he can more easily ignore your one-hand tactic.

While you are training your horse to double, you should be teaching the horse to yield to the bit (see p. 43). That is why it is important to double against a barrier high enough that he cannot get his head over the top of it — to get him in the habit of keeping his nose down as well as shifting his balance to the rear. With the bosal hackamore, you have had it if the horse sticks his nose up in the air. That's why the vaqueros took such great pains to teach the colt to tuck to the jáquima (hackamore). It isn't quite

Control the runaway horse by doubling him the moment he thinks about bolting — or even when he disobeys you by trying to go faster than you want.

so vital with the ordinary snaffle bit, but the quicker you get the horse to yield to it, the better control you will have and the better able the horse will be to stop immediately and in balance.

A horse yields to the jáquima or bit when he relaxes his jaw and neck muscles and tucks his nose back slightly — not necessarily when his face is in the vertical. He makes the contact soft. Encourage him to keep it that way by driving him forward as you maintain a definite but elastic feel with the reins. *Never pull* on the reins to try to get the horse to tuck his nose. If you don't pull, the horse won't set his jaw and pull on you. We always hear of the horse taking the bit in his teeth to run away. I am convinced this doesn't happen — instead the horse sticks his nose out or up and stiffens his jaw and neck into a solid-brick-wall effect. If he does this because pain has blanked out his mind or something has triggered his mental trauma on the subject, nothing you can do will unlock those muscles once he is off and running.

There are all sorts of gimmicks used to make a horse tuck his nose, but only the most sensitive of riders should use them on spoiled horses. Such riders should be able to get a colt to yield without gimmicks because there is always danger of getting a horse behind the bit through their use. A horse that is behind the bit — tucks his nose too far, in order to drop contact — can do exactly as he pleases. If you have trouble with these things, go back to Chapters 3 and 4 and study how to teach a horse to double, yield to the bit, and stop.

This is the order of training a horse to stop after you have taught him to double and while you are teaching him to yield. Concurrently teach him to stop from the walk and to come down to the walk from the trot. When he is doing these well, teach him to stop from the trot and to come down to the trot from the canter. If the horse will readily change from canter to trot, you do not have to be able to stop him easily from the canter to control him. The stop from the canter is more difficult for the horse and requires more preparatory training to get it without causing other problems.

Initially ask the horse to yield after each stop, but don't keep doing it after he has learned to come to a stop already yielded

First get the horse to yield to the bit and then ask for the transition (change of gait) up or down.

because that can get him going behind the bit. When asking for any transitions (changes of gait up or down), first get the horse to yield and then ask. Naturally, you will double him or grind him to a walk or halt without worrying about the yielding if he tries to run away, but other than that, get him in the habit of being soft on the bit at all times.

Some horses think when you ask for the canter that it is an invitation to run. You can help a horse get over this notion by cantering only about 100 feet at a time, bringing him down to the trot and walk before cantering again. When he starts wanting to break back to the trot of his own accord at that distance, start varying it so he becomes convinced that he canters and trots at your command — not at his pleasure.

Some things are important if you want to develop and maintain a good saddle horse. One is that you never race your horse because that makes him foolish. Don't canter him home — walk the last eighth of a mile — and don't run for fun. When your horse canters under control, you can ask for speed by pushing him into longer strides. This gives you a controlled gallop, but just kicking him into an excited run teaches him to run out of control. Avoid the temptation to try gymkhana or stock horse "routines" before you have spent months and months advancing the horse's training in a logical order. Avoid riding with "two-gaiters" (prancy walk and dead run). Ignoring these precautions encourages your horse to become a runaway.

I have been told that giving a horse goodies and/or unsaddling him immediately at the end of a ride will make him barnsour. Some people suggest taking a little grain along to feed to the horse out on the trail to cure homesickness. I have tried these things and found that the obedient horse leaves home willingly and comes back quietly regardless. Goodies and immediate unsaddling reward a horse for a good ride. Leaving a spoiled horse saddled and tied for an hour or two at the end of a bad ride can improve his attitude — but not without the accompaniment of retraining.

One person wrote that her horse ran away with her and when she got him stopped, she whipped him. The next time she rode him, he ran away again, farther and faster. Her horse believed that he was punished for stopping, so he naturally was more reluctant to stop the next time. You can't punish a horse by whipping him while he is running away either, because that just tells him to go that much faster. You have to avoid runaways by training the horse at home to be obedient — completely obedient — to your slowing and stopping aids.

When you can easily bring your horse down from a canter to a trot and easily stop him from a trot, you are ready to ride him out on the trails again. You can always double him in an emergency. Keep him moving forward in the walk and trot, reminding him to pay attention to you by closing your legs firmly each time his attention wanders. Avoid the canter until you are sure he is

Leaving a spoiled horse saddled and tied at the end of a bad ride can help improve his attitude in some cases.

obedient in the walk and trot. Be definite in asking what you want of the horse; don't let him make the decisions as to gait, speed, and direction.

I have heard repeatedly that the way to cure a runaway is to take him out and run him. That's sheer nonsense — it's natural for horses to like to run, and the more you run them the more they will want to run. Pi Dough is a good example. As a colt he couldn't lope as fast as my husband's small horse could walk, so Bill suggested that I run him some each time I rode him. I did this one day too many and Pi Dough decided to go all out. Even though I was able to control him, after that he would sometimes make a bid to run when we cantered.

At that time we moved from the flat land to the mountains and I made use of the terrain to handle the situation. If you canter a colt or a spoiled horse up a long, medium slope, it will control the speed and the distance of the run without your having to pull on the reins. When you feel the horse wanting to break back to the trot, you can push him a stride or two farther and then ask for the trot so he thinks you have complete control of his canter. This procedure lets you control the horse without having to double him excessively. Psychologically, it makes him think you have control of him in the gallop — and after all, all training must be your mind over his matter since he has a lot more mass than you do.

Some people have trouble with horses that take them into the barn or that duck out the gate of the riding arena. Until you have gained control, close the barn doors and the arena gate. Always dismount to take your horse into the barn. Whenever you open the arena gate to ride out, continue riding in the arena until the horse will go in a relaxed walk — *then* you can ride through the gate. Vary where you ride during this walking around because horses are very clever at learning a pattern and when it is time to bolt out the gate. I ride past the gate a time or two, sometimes stopping at the gate and riding on in the arena, sometimes dismounting there and leading the horse out. The horse must never be quite sure when I am going to ask him to go through the gate. This encourages his obedience.

7

Prancing

If I had to take my choice between a confirmed prancer and a confirmed rearer, I think I would take the rearing horse as long as he wasn't a smashing success at it. As dangerous as rearing is, it is much easier to cure than prancing. A horse that prances will revert to it any time he gets excited about going when you want him to walk. The favorite direction is toward home. I once spent two hours on what should have been a half-hour trip home, trying to get a confirmed prancer to walk at least part of the way. Her name, appropriately enough, was Bubbles; and I think they were the soap variety because we were both in a lather by the time we made it home.

Some people seem to like prancing, thinking that it shows the horse has spirit. When Bubbles was for sale, some folks rode her around the yard to try her out. Even though she performed quietly and obediently for these people, they weren't sure she suited them and they came back for a second look. This time Bubbles bubbled all over the place and that was that. They enthusiastically bought her! I couldn't believe it! The saying, "I don't know what he sees in her" can apply to more than human affairs.

The best time to cure prancing is when it first begins. Iam was about three the first time he tried it. I didn't have time that day for a long ride so I just made a circle ride close to home. Usually Iam would rather go anywhere but home, but his buddies had just come down from the hills so I guess he was anxious to get back and visit with them. Anyway, when I turned him toward

The prancing horse is a pain in more ways than one. This is neither willingness to go forward nor spirit.

home, he wanted to rush off. When I tried to make him walk, he put all of his still-fresh energy into trying to prance.

No matter how little time you have, you must take time to stop a bad habit the moment it starts. Iam wouldn't respond to my sitting relaxed and driving him forward and I knew that just holding him back would make him prance more. Doubling prevents runaways but doesn't prevent prancing in the least. I just trotted him around and around in a large circle, one direction for a while and then the other, until he stopped trying to rush toward home and to slow down each time we headed away from home. When he finally settled into a relaxed rhythm at the trot, I asked him to walk home, pushing him forward in a definite walk rhythm.

I think it was about a year later Iam tried one more time to rush home. This time he was much farther along in his training and all I had to do was sit relaxed and maintain a strong walking rhythm. Iam's basic training is sound — I make him work with energy without exciting him. Lots of horses are taught to prance because their owners confuse excitement with energetic output. Then they try to control their excited horses with a strong, steady pull on the reins and the horses prance.

The reason prancing is so hard to cure is that it takes a

great amount of feel, reflex action, and controlled relaxation on the part of the rider. The horse wants to rush off in a trot or gallop, so you have to hold him to control him. But holding him tightly with the reins makes him nervous and he prances more. If your legs touch his sides, he spurts ahead; but pushing your legs away from his body makes your body tense, which makes him more nervous, so he prances more. The horse keeps jostling you forward and back in fits and starts, and probably throws in some head tossing. You can't decide which is worse — letting him take off in a dead run or holding him to this uncontrolled "walk."

The first thing you must do is relax. You must sit up tall with your head up, let your shoulders drop down and back, let your legs rest on the horse's sides, and your feet rest in the stirrups. Most important of all, you must stay relaxed in the waist so your seat can go with every movement of the horse. Your fingers must relax to invite the horse to relax, closing only for an instant each time he spurts ahead. This means you must feel the horse so well that you can practically read his thoughts. It is only through feel and reflex action that you can capitalize on each hint that the horse will relax.

When you are relaxed, you can feel the horse better and can react more appropriately to him. But it is very difficult to relax on

Think of relaxing as just sitting there no matter what the horse does.

By controlling the horse with flexible fingers and a firm walking rhythm (set by your seat), you can get the horse to walk — as Pi Dough is doing now — instead of prance.

a prancing horse. Think of it as just sitting there no matter what he does. When you have achieved this relaxation, you will find that his wiggles don't jiggle you so much.

There are two things you must feel — the horse's offer to relax his jaw and neck, and his offer to take a walking stride. You must be constantly relaxing your fingers to invite the horse to relax his jaw and neck. At each hint of relaxation, you must yield your fingers, and even your arms, forward more without losing contact. Any necessary holding must be very brief. This must be reflex action because you must also concentrate on catching any offer the horse makes to walk. At each little offer to take a walk stride, try to pick up a walk rhythm and maintain it. Regardless of the jostling, you must relax your waist and you must keep your seat and pelvis going in a strong walking rhythm just as if the horse were truly walking.

When the horse eventually picks up your walking rhythm, you must keep him walking forward by pushing each seatbone a little farther forward on each side than the horse takes it but not so much that you push him into a trot. You must relax the reins enough so that he will start to lower his head and stay relaxed but not so much that he breaks into a trot. And through it all you must stay relaxed yourself so you don't make the horse more tense with your tension.

If you live in brush country and the brush is high enough and thick enough to impede the horse's progress, you can make use

Tall brush can discourage
a horse from prancing or
rushing toward home.

of it to control the homesick horse without having to pull on his mouth. It needs to be a long enough stretch of brush so your horse can see the error of his ways before he gets out in the open. Head him into the brush and let him go. Guide him only enough to keep him in it and yourself out of trouble. Let the horse figure out for himself that rushing home isn't profitable. If one trip through isn't enough, bring him around and let him do it again and again until he comes out ready to drop his head and walk home. Chaps and a denim jacket are recommended for this trip.

I can't guarantee a complete cure if the horse's prancing is a well-established habit. When Pi Dough was three he was ridden for a month by a fellow who taught him to prance. I immediately taught him not to prance, but now at nineteen he still reverts to it when he hasn't been ridden regularly. It takes about 200 yards to get him walking when I turn toward home, but he doesn't give me any trouble with prancing when he's ridden regularly. I hate Pi Dough's prancing but bless him for helping me learn how to change it to walking.

8

Rearing

It is an interesting challenge to try to give a person valid advice on how to cure his horse problems when all I have to go on is his letter, but it can also be frustrating. I have to find all the clues I can in the letter and relate them to all my experience in order to identify the true problem and its cause and so come up with its cure. I love "whodunits," but I'm no Sherlock Holmes who is able to read the whole story from a single hair from the tail of the horse that misbehaves. Of course, if the person knew what information I needed, he might also know what to try to cure the problem; so I can't blame him if his letter is rather vague. One such letter read as follows:

> I have a six-year-old Morgan. All summer he was very well be-haved. Then when winter came, I couldn't ride him at all. The ground was so bad. So I moved him to a new stable. Now this March, he thinks he's supposed to be in the barn all the time. When I take him out, he tries to go back in the barn. If I don't let him, he rears up high — and I mean high! There's nothing I can do to make him go where I want. I never gave him his way. How can I stop him from rearing?

From that letter I could not tell for sure whether the girl was riding or leading her horse out of the barn. There was no indication that the horse had been out of the barn all winter, so that suggested that he might have gone stir-crazy. I wrote to Debbie, trying to cover all possibilities, but mainly explaining to her that a horse cannot rear when he is going forward. I told her that she must make the horse move, then immediately guide him away from the barn and keep him moving.

About three months later I got a letter from Debbie telling me what terrible advice I had given her; that if she had followed it, she still would not be riding her horse. She told me that the stableman where she boards her horse had ridden him out and every time the horse reared, he had hit him over the head. Now, she said, she could ride her horse anywhere — even bareback with a halter.

I published the gist of her letter and answered it with a letter addressed to "Dear Debbie's Horse." I apologized in the letter for failing him and pointed out (for the benefit of my readers) that this is a dangerous method of curing rearing and quite the improper way to go about it. I sympathized with Debbie's Horse and pointed out to him how lucky it was that he had given up so easily or he might have been injured, blinded, or killed. I explained that I know horses are masters at thinking up ways to get out of work, and I added that I wished people would realize that most of a horse's shenanigans can be cured simply by training him to go forward freely and relaxed.

I thought I had been rather clever in writing to Debbie's Horse to point out the errors of the stableman's ways rather than chewing him out directly. Guess what happened! I received a vitriolic letter from a girl who said she was in the process of curing her horse of rearing by hitting him over the head. She raked me over the coals for everything from my "childish, unrealistic" pen name to my age, which she guessed as 45 and the proper age for mandatory retirement. In the middle of all this she told me how dumb I was to think that moving a horse forward would cure his rearing. I published the more printable parts of her letter, merely mentioning in rebuttal that I am over 30 and therefore cannot be trusted.

This brought me a flood of mail. Not only did my readers stand up for me personally (which made me feel good), but letter after letter told of maimed and dead horses that had been hit over the head for rearing. The top of a horse's head is where his brain is; and while a horse may seem pretty hard-headed at times, no horse has an iron skull. One letter told of a trainer who got fed up with a young stallion that reared every time he rode him past other horses. This man hit the colt on the head with the wooden handle of a twitch. The colt staggered and dropped to his knees, with blood gushing from his mouth. Luckily, the only permanent damage he suffered was the loss of two front teeth.

In another case, as a girl mounted her new Thoroughbred hunter, he reared and she promptly cracked him on the head with her crop. The horse reared again and fell over backward, hitting his head on the mounting block. This horse spent the next four months in his stall, blind in both eyes, hardly eating — just standing there with his head lowered, grinding his teeth or bumping into the walls. They finally had him put down. While it may have been freaky that the horse hit his head on the mounting block, I have received many letters telling of horses that reared when hit over the head with something as innocuous as a riding crop.

My critic stated that people are not as dumb as I must think — that they would know better than to use a club or weapon to hit a rearing horse on the head. I have learned that some people *are* that dumb, as the Twitch-Handle Case proves. Further proof is the Beer Bottle Case, which involved another young stallion that reared habitually. One day the owner and some of his buddies sat down and polished off a case of beer. The owner then proceeded to break the empty beer bottles over the stallion's head in an effort to cure his rearing. Amazingly, the horse escaped injury or death. He finally escaped further mistreatment when he was sold to an understanding horseman who cured his rearing by training him to go forward willingly. Another girl wrote,

I own a nine-year-old Morgan mare that also had the bad habit of rearing. When I bought her two years ago, she was almost impossible to ride. I received a lot of bad advice from some so-called "horse trainers." Among their remedies were such things as breaking soft drink bottles filled with sand between the ears (just think what that would do to a horse!), using the end of a hunt crop, and even using a two-by-four. Fortunately I was experienced enough to know the dangers of such practices, but it makes me sick to think of all the inexperienced riders that follow such dangerous advice. And this does happen because I personally know of people who have tried these inhumane methods.

One woman did write in disagreement. She had recently bought a horse, mainly for jumping but also because he was supposed to be a good trail horse. This was a nine-year-old horse that was supposed to be well trained. He went well on the trail with other horses; but when his owner took him out alone, he went just so far and then gave her quite a tussle — first by rearing when he was asked to go forward and then by running backward on a loose rein. Since he would not go forward, she tried to punish him by backing him. Twice he set his jaw and tried to run home. When she got him turned around, he started rearing again.

She told me that she finally solved this problem by "clouting him on the head" with a stout stick when he reared. It took three sessions of clouting before she felt he was going forward obediently enough to take him home. She concluded by saying, "I don't think this lesson with obviously successful results should be irrevocably condemned."

I do irrevocably condemn it. If this rider had understood how to handle a rearing horse correctly, she could have shown that horse in short order that he had to go forward with her. It would have saved both of them a headache.

Rearing is a dangerous habit. People have been killed and crippled riding rearing horses. If a horse rears suddenly, he can lose his balance and fall back or he can rear so violently that he actually throws himself back on the ground with force. If you lose your balance and use the reins to keep from falling, you can pull the horse over; or you can cause the horse to fall simply by upsetting his balance with your displaced weight. When a horse rears with you, always lean forward immediately and move your hands forward to give him plenty of rein. Put your arms around his neck if necessary, and let go of the reins if you must slide off.

I have heard that you can bring a horse back to earth by grabbing one rein close to his mouth and pulling down and out. I have never tried it but have the feeling that the person could easily unbalance the horse and find *himself* down and out. I have also read that the way to cure a horse of rearing is to slide off and pull him over while he is still up in the air. If you aren't able to train a horse to go forward willingly — the safest and most effective prevention and cure for rearing — how are you going to manage to get out of the way as you attempt to pull him over? I would rather be unnoticed and safe than spectacular and sorry.

The whole idea behind hitting a horse over the head when he rears is to punish him and make him think he has bumped his head on something. I have seen horses hit their heads and go right back and do it again in the same place, in the same way, so that theory doesn't hold water. If you are going to punish a horse, it should be done where it will get to his brain through his nervous system, not directly through his skull. It is necessary to know how to punish a horse correctly, but it is even more important to know what position a horse must be in to do things. Then you can put him in position to get the performance you want — and keep him out of position to pull the disobedience you do not want.

Basically, the horse that tries to rear during handling is the one whose style of playing includes a lot of rearing. Occasionally, a horse that has never given his rider a hint of rearing can be crowded into it. My daughter had such an experience while warming up her horse with a group for cavalletti class. Roufus had been schooled for about four years and had never tried to rear. During this warm-up with horses coming at him from all angles, he suddenly stood up on his hind legs and walked several strides. Betty said she had the feeling that Roufus felt threatened by the other horses and unable to escape by going forward, so the only place left to go was up.

Another incident of a well-trained horse unexpectedly rearing ended disastrously. The girl was riding out on a trail when she came across some cows in the brush. Her horse was not accustomed to cows and wanted to whirl to run away from them. The girl held him between her legs and hands to keep him from whirling and to try to get him to move toward the cows. Her horse was obedient (even though greatly frightened), but he finally couldn't stand the strain and reared so high that he lost his balance and fell on the girl. She suffered broken bones that took some time to heal, but she was wise enough to understand that she had held her obedient horse trapped until fear had overpowered him.

A horse rears by exerting his energy upward instead of forward. As we have just seen, he may rear because he feels it is his only escape route. In many cases a horse starts rearing because he has no choice — his rider tells him to go forward vigorously while holding him back strongly with the reins. Or he may start rearing from the pain of having his mouth jerked (although his first reaction to that is to throw his head up). The combination of pain and confusion from strong conflicting aids is the most common cause of rearing.

Horses that rear naturally in play will often use it as a defense against putting out energy to work. A rider with a good feel of the horse will usually feel such a horse get light in front and so can stop this dangerous habit before it starts. A horse must stop in order to rear, so it follows that the way to prevent rearing is to move him forward with energy. If you are definite about this each time you feel the horse get light in front, and give him a place to go forward as you ask, your horse will not rear under any ordinary circumstances.

My Frosty filly was a potential rearer. When she resisted going forward, I could feel her get light in front as if she would rear if I didn't keep her going better. One day as I was starting out on a ride with my daughter, Frosty decided she didn't want to leave the yard and without warning stood straight up on her hind legs. I instinctively leaned forward onto her neck as I gave her completely loose rein — the only safe thing to do whenever a horse rears. When her front feet were almost back to the ground, I booted her forward, *hard,* and headed her for the side of the barn. There I doubled her and booted her out, then doubled her back the other way and booted her right on past the barn. Then I firmly said "Ho" as I closed my legs and hands. She stopped obediently. Then I simply closed my legs again and she obediently walked on away from home.

If a horse takes you by surprise and actually does rear, be sure to leave the reins loose as you suddenly and explosively *drive him forward* — just as his front feet are going to touch the ground. At that time he is committed to coming down and would find it difficult to rear again suddenly.

By being so sudden and so strong with the driving aids, you

"goose" the horse into moving forward. The doubling changes the horse's mind about being disobedient. If there isn't anything to double against, double in the open. As I said earlier, every horse should be trained to double (see Chapter 3). Always stay very alert with a horse that rears and keep him moving forward obediently and with energy. A horse must stop to rear even though the stop may be so brief that you are not aware of it.

Some horses become so thoroughly "trained" to rear by riders who try to make them go forward on too tight a rein that they will even rear on a completely loose rein when told to go anywhere they don't want to go. The woman who took the stout stick to clout her horse over the head had found herself on such a horse. I heard of a horse that would rear and throw himself if the rider so much as closed his legs on him. Just sitting on this horse was dangerous, so his latest rider cured him by ground-driving him and using a voice command each time he drove the horse forward sharply with the whip. Then the rider used the voice command while mounted, until the horse would go forward obediently under saddle and subsequently learned to accept the rider's legs. The whole thing is to get the horse to go forward willingly so he cannot stop and rear.

This sounds simple, but rearing gets started in a variety of circumstances because riders do not understand what is going on at those times. A friend of mine rode his filly over to my house. It was her first ride away from home and he explained to me that he had just walked her and had no trouble as long as they were on the road, which she naturally followed. When they took a shortcut across open country, she didn't want to go that way and tried to rear when he tried to make her.

Bud was making some serious mistakes. He rode his filly out on the trail before he had her trotting and doubling. He was not using a leading rein to help her turn. A young horse should be trained in all these things before being ridden out, so you can avoid the beginning of bad habits such as rearing. It is easier for a horse to hold back in the walk than in the trot, and a horse that gets sticky about going forward is harder to control and guide. It is just like trying to turn the wheels of a truck when it is standing still. The momentum of the trot makes it harder for a horse to

Iam goes forward willingly, yields to the bit, and understands the aids. This sort of good basic training is the best way to prevent and cure bad habits.

use his strength against you, and doubling gives you control in an emergency. You can get the horse to turn with the leading rein, without pulling back and confusing him into rearing, bucking, and other kinds of resistance. Especially with a young horse, it is foolish to invite problems by trusting to luck instead of education.

Bud does know enough to train his filly to go forward and to use a snaffle bit on her. Quite often the people who have troubles with young horses rearing mention that they are using a curb bit of some sort. Remember that a mechanical hackamore and the so-called western snaffle are curb bits. It is impossible to avoid having to pull a colt around at times just to get obedience. If you are using a curb bit of any kind, you are inviting the colt to rear. Even with the true snaffle you can hurt a colt's mouth enough that it might rear, so turn it with a leading rein and do more kicking than pulling.

Some colts start rearing simply because they are too young to be ridden. Others start this bad habit because your training confuses them. Either you don't explain what you want in a way they can understand, or you ask for so many things at once that they can't understand any of them. If you try to force a horse to yield to the bit, you can make him rear. If you ride a horse beyond his endurance, he may start rearing with you.

Some people have written that they tried a tiedown to prevent rearing. Apparently it may have helped in one or two cases, but shortening it enough to discourage rearing can make some horses feel so stuck in a bind that they start bucking. At any rate, a tiedown brands the rider as one who would rather force his horse to accept his rough hands and severe bit than educate himself in the art of handling the reins and the horse intelligently and sympathetically.

Another girl who was advised to hit her horse between the ears with a board when he reared knew that this could be hazardous to his health, so she used her crop on his head instead. He promptly went berserk and dumped her. A week later she got up enough nerve to try riding him again. This time she just turned him in short circles every time he thought of rearing. It took several rides, but she did cure him of rearing. Turning the horse in tight circles will work almost as well as doubling if you keep your hand low and out to the side to turn him. It keeps him off-balance and moving until you can get him to relax and go forward again.

You can get a lot of advice of all sorts on problems. One girl wrote that she had been told to pull down when a horse reared and lift up when he bucked. She was in trouble because her horse would rear when she pulled up and buck when she pulled down. How much simpler to understand that the horse could not do either one when he was going forward willingly!

Some horses rear because they don't want to go forward, such as the horse that doesn't want to leave home or cross a stream or bridge. Others rear because they *do* want to go and are being held back severely, such as the excited horse whose rider tries to hold him to a standstill. These horses are not obedient, but a well-trained horse that suddenly starts rearing could have a sore mouth. The mouth is the first thing to check in that case — then check the bit to see if it has developed rough edges and the curb strap or chain to see if it is pinching anywhere. Sometimes the well-trained horse can be simply feeling his oats — like the time I was graining up my mare for a show. She saw some horses in the distance and enthusiastically stood right up on her hind legs. Don't you know she got cut back at the feed bag!

One girl wrote to me about her "otherwise quite good" seven-year-old pony:

Whenever I ride him in a circle, he rears and bucks and gets me out of balance. Then he tries to run away. I've managed to make him walk in a circle but not more than seven times around. The circle is about twenty feet and I use a curb bit.

A twenty-foot circle is small even for a pony, and trying to force him to stay on it with a curb bit could make him fight the pain with the reaction the girl describes. If the girl would ride her pony in a circle no smaller than 40 feet in diameter and use a snaffle bit so she could control him without hurting him, her problems of rearing, bucking, and running away would be solved. This is a good example of an otherwise well-behaved

Rules for this trail class: Horses to cross the bridge singly. This normally obedient horse wants to go with his buddy and is being told not to, so he is getting light in front.

This kind of firm but sympathetic handling of a scary situation will prevent rearing or other problems.

After competing in one speed event, this pony threatened to rear and balk at the start of each of the following events. The young rider handled the situation well and avoided trouble, but better basic training would help even more.

equine acting up just because he is asked to perform beyond his present capability.

And here is one I am not sure about. Priscilla writes,

> I have a problem with Blackfoot, my Morgan horse. Every time I come to a hill he rears up. I try to make him go up, but he always rears. So I have to get off and lead him up. What can I do?

It is a cinch that Blackfoot now has Priscilla's number when it comes to hills, but what made him start to refuse to go up them in the first place? My guess is that he wanted to run up them, which is natural for any horse that isn't strong enough yet to walk up. Priscilla tried to make him walk up by taking a very strong hold on the reins. Then he either was frustrated by being told to go up the hill while being told at the same time not to go at all, or he went bounding up the hill anyway, hurting his mouth on every bound. Whatever the cause, he is just like all the rest — he needs a home-study course in going forward obediently under control.

Some rearing is a by-product of other problems, and I will deal with that at appropriate times (see Chapter 15). The main thing to understand about preventing and curing this dangerous habit is that you must train the horse to go forward obediently, and if he does rear, you can control him while keeping him moving by doubling or by turning him in tight circles with your hand low and out to the side. This must be done with an ordinary snaffle because any curb bit can hurt him enough to make him rear more. When a horse is standing up on his hind legs, the rider is helpless. At that point the only safe thing to do is to lean forward on the horse's neck and give him a loose rein. Then drive him forward when his front feet are nearly down to the ground.

There is one other thing of importance. Do not train your horse to rear. Except for true balking, rearing is a horse's most effective defense against working for you. Since a horse can use acquired knowledge as well as instinctive actions to avoid having to work, why give him such useful knowledge?

The horses at the Spanish Riding School that are taught the *levade* (a rear in the classical statue pose) are first given an advanced course of instruction so they are very responsive to whatever their riders ask. The movie-TV horses that are taught to rear are trained in obedience from the very beginning and are then trained to rear only on cue. None of these horses are ordinary saddle horses — they are used for special purposes.

It is inadvisable to train your horse to rear.

There are riders who are capable of handling their trained rearing horses quite well. If you have taught your horse to rear and then decide that you want to sell him, be sure to explain to prospective buyers not only that he has this training but also the problems it can cause. Riders that are inexperienced or not so brave can be seriously injured by such a horse no matter how gentle he is. The best thing is to avoid all such problems by foregoing such training.

9

Standing Quietly

Standing for mounting

Thirty-five or so years ago when I had owned horses for only about five years, I also owned a few milk goats. At the time, I was pasturing them about two miles from home and riding my mare to the pasture every day to milk the one goat that wasn't dry yet. I used a little tin pail with a tight lid for the milk, and my mare normally didn't care at all when my hand and that pail together would grab the horn as I mounted — except on this one day.

As I got ready to mount, Mother and I had some conversation. The mare must have dozed off while waiting. Conversation over, I shoved my foot in the stirrup as I grabbed the horn with the pail in my hand. The mare leaped into a gallop. There I was with my foot wedged in the stirrup, hanging at arm's length from the saddle horn. With the road rushing past my head, I somehow found the strength to pull myself up and into the saddle. I slowed the mare down to a trot and waved at Mother half a block behind to show her that I was okay.

It's amazing what strength we have in an emergency. It's also amazing what kind of advice we can get from some "experts." Somewhere just recently I read some instructions on mounting that said to put your foot deep into the stirrup. This is a very dangerous practice. If I had known that day years ago (as I later learned) to put just my toe in the stirrup, my foot would have slipped out the moment the mare leaped ahead; and I wouldn't have scared myself and my mother half to death. If that gentle mare could be startled into running, think how much more important it is for you to mount safely if you have problems getting your horse to stand for mounting. Be sure to put just your toe in the stirrup when trying to mount. It's the only safe way for anyone to mount. (Better get your horse's attention, too!)

I find a tendency among riders to consider each problem as an isolated one that is unrelated to the rest of the horse's behavior. In some cases this can be true, but most problems that show up are complicated by other ones that make the solving of the specific one difficult. For example, a horse that won't stand for mounting may not be obedient to the command "Ho" when he is being led or ridden. The horse that is kept excited during riding won't be in any frame of mind to stand quietly when the rider is trying to mount. I recommend tying a horse up to train him to stand for mounting because this gives the rider one less thing to coordinate. Some horses won't stand tied, so this creates a problem in solving the present one. I have told you how to ride your horse to relax him and how to train him to stop. I will deal with leading and tying up problems later on, in Chapter 15.

The first step in training or retraining any horse is to have him under control. This statement probably frustrates you, because lack of control is the reason you are having trouble with mounting. For control in this case tie your horse up in a *safe* place — to a strong post in a board fence or to a tree beside a board fence. (Never tie a horse to a weak rail in a board fence, or to anything he could pull over on himself.) If your horse tries to

For safety, mount and dismount with only your toe in the stirrup.

crowd you against the fence when you try to mount him, he should first be thoroughly trained to move away from you. Do this by tapping him on his side to make him move his haunches away. At first you may have to take his head toward you to get him to move over. Do this on both sides every time you groom him. When you lead him through gates, don't just pull his head around to turn him back so you can close the gate — tap him on the side to make him move his haunches away from you. Get him to be thoroughly obedient to this.

Tie your horse up with a strong halter and rope. I tie my rope into the halter, because almost all snaps are weak. Certainly you don't want to crowd your horse into pulling back and breaking loose, but you must always be prepared for the worst. Tie the horse (with a quick-release knot, for safety) at about his eye level when his head is at rest and have about 18 inches of tie rope between the post and the halter.

Start training your horse to stand still for mounting at the end of each ride, when he isn't so anxious to get going. His reaction determines how fast you can proceed with the training. If he has fits the moment you reach for the stirrup and pommel, your first move is to get him to accept these movements. Whatever you do, don't pet him when he jumps around, thinking to calm him. Simply stand there until he is still; *then* pet him. This way you can gradually get him to accept your reaching for the stirrup and the horn.

The next step is to put your toe — just your toe — in the stirrup, then to stand in the stirrup balanced over the horse's back, and finally to swing your leg over to sit in the saddle. Stay in position in each of these steps until the horse stands still before you go on to the next step. If you just go ahead and mount regardless of what he does, you won't teach him to stand quietly for mounting.

Tying your horse up for this kind of training relieves you of having to use your mind and muscle to try to keep him in one small area. He can still move around some whether he is tied or you are holding the reins. When he moves, don't back off unless you are in danger. If you jump back or off every time he moves, you will just confirm his bad habit. If he starts moving

If the horse moves at any stage of mounting, stay in position until he stands still.

when you put your toe in the stirrup, hop with him until he stands. If he moves as you are going up, stay balanced over his back until he stands. If he moves as you sit down in the saddle, just sit there relaxed until he stands. During your riding, never let him move off of his own accord — stop him and make him stand until *you* tell him to move.

The way you mount has a lot to do with getting your horse to stand still. If you poke him with your toe or bump him as you swing your leg over his back, you are telling him to move. If you hang on the saddle to pull yourself up, he will feel that he should move to maintain his balance. If you thump down in the saddle, that hurts his back and makes him inclined to move around. Take note of these things and retrain yourself if it's needed. Your horse shouldn't have to learn to stand in spite of its being uncomfortable for him.

When the horse will stand for mounting tied up, add the bridle so you can take contact with the near rein only. This contact isn't to make him hold still but to give you a way to tighten the rein briefly to tell him to stand. If he steps back when you pick up the contact, it is too strong. Get him to let you mount while you have contact with his mouth on that near rein. When he begins to accept this mounting at the end of your rides, mount him this way at the beginning, using a snap on the halter so you can unsnap it to go about your riding. When he is thoroughly obedient about standing for mounting when he's tied up, mount him

When the horse stands
still, continue mounting.

at this same place without tying him at the beginning of each
ride. Practice mounting at other places around home at the end
of your rides.

When your horse will stand while you mount anywhere
around home, start training him out on the trail. Do this in the
latter part of a ride and choose places where it will be easy for
you to mount. It helps to head the horse away from home while
you mount so he won't be quite so anxious to get going. It also
helps to have him stand in a slight dip in the ground so you don't
have to reach so far to get your foot in the stirrup. As a safety
measure, always take contact with the near rein, even after he is
thoroughly trained to stand anywhere for mounting. Then if he
moves for any reason, he will tend to move in a circle around
you and this will help you get on his back instead of leaving you
in the dust to walk home.

Recently I was told that a better way to get a horse to stand is
to take up contact on the off rein instead of the near rein. The
theory behind this is that if the horse tries to move, he will swing
his body into the person mounting, think he is up against an
obstacle, and therefore stand still. The one horse I tried this on is
neither impolite nor wild about moving around, so he did stand
when he moved his body into mine. However, I have met up

with several horses that would just as soon shove me down and dance a jig on top of me, so I wouldn't think of trying this on one of them. Whichever rein you use, you have to train the horse to stand — you can't just hold him still with the reins.

Short people who ride tall horses and people who ride bareback often have a problem getting a horse to stand for mounting. I teach all my horses to stand alongside anything I choose so I will never find myself in a situation where I wouldn't be able to mount. Probably all of you have tried at one time or another to mount from a fence or a stump only to have the horse turn his body away out of your reach. It tries one's patience to try to get such a horse to stay alongside the stump or fence long enough for you to get in position and mount the horse. But there is a way that you can train a horse to do this.

Using a short whip, I train the horse on the ground to move his hindquarters away from me and toward me. Stand beside the horse's head on his left facing his rear. As you take a little on the halter rope to turn the horse's head just slightly toward you, tap him on the side of his haunches. Make each separate tap a little harder until he moves his hindquarters away from the tap. Immediately lower the whip, release your hold on the halter rope, and pet him. Repeat this until he moves his hindquarters away when you point the whip at them.

Next go to the off side and train him to move away from the tap of the whip on that side. In the third lesson, after reviewing

Pi Dough moves his hindquarters away from the whip.

these two lessons, reach across the horse's back from the near side to tap the horse's hip on the off side with the whip. He should move his hindquarters toward you. Sometimes it takes two or three hard taps to get him to realize this means the same as your standing on his off side to tap him.

When the horse will move his hindquarters toward you whenever you point the whip across his hips, lead him up to the fence (or whatever) head first. Get up on the fence and use the whip signal to get him to move his hindquarters toward you until he is lined up parallel to the fence so you can mount. Eventually all you will have to do is snap your fingers across his back to get him to line up beside whatever mounting block you choose. I train my horses to respond from either side for convenience.

This training also helps a horse learn to stand for mounting under any circumstances although it won't completely do the job. It's a great help if you're trying to get your horse to stand so you can mount him bareback. One thing bareback mounters should avoid at all times is poking the horse with an elbow or knee. This is one reason why the horse moves around.

If a horse has been trained to take off at a gallop the moment your foot touches the stirrup, you just have to retrain him patiently and consistently over a long period of time. If your horse tries to bite or kick you during mounting, make sure there aren't any tender places on his back or under the cinch. Anything that makes mounting — or riding — painful or disagreeable to the horse can make him fight back when you try to mount. If nothing is hurting him, let your feet come back to the ground and swat him as hard as you can with the flat of your hand on the side of his belly when he tries to bite or kick. Immediately step back up to him and start the mounting procedure again. At all times you must be boss and this sudden, just punishment shows him you are.

Punishment should never be over-used, and some kinds should never be used at all for various reasons. Bert was starting some eight-year-old Standardbred mares that had been running on the range. One of these mares would consistently take off at a run when he mounted. One time he rode her up under a tree and tied the end of the lead rope to a limb, thinking it would keep her

Pointing the whip across his hips causes Pi Dough to move his hindquarters toward me — the end result of proper training.

Pi Dough stands beside my mounting block as I mount, using all safety precautions even though he is well trained.

standing until he was mounted again and could untie it. That bright idea produced nothing but bright lights, since the mare leaped into a run the second his seat hit the saddle. When she hit the end of the lead rope, it doubled her and launched Bert into space. Unfortunately for him, it wasn't endless space, but at least he learned what not to try.

Bill was successful with a similar cure. The horse he was riding would always bolt for home every time Bill tried to mount him after going through a certain gate. So Bill armed himself with a long lead rope which he tied around the horse's neck and to the base of the gate post. As the horse made his leap away from this starting gate, Bill just stepped back out of the way. When the horse hit the end of the rope, he threw himself flat with a thud that knocked the wind out of him. It cured him of ever trying again, but this sort of drastic cure is hard on the equipment and could be fatal to the horse. Consistent, patient training may take time; but it is safer for everyone concerned.

Standing quietly under saddle

If your horse won't stand quietly under saddle, you can work on this while you are training him to stand for mounting. There are three things to remember, and these apply to his mounting training too. If you try to hold the horse still with the reins, he will be uncomfortable and unable to relax and will either step toward the rear or move around anxiously. If you try to keep him from backing by tightening the reins — an automatic reaction since that's the way you tell him to "ho" when he's moving forward — he will back that much more. If you don't relax yourself, and act convincingly as if you have all the time in the world (whether you do or not), your horse will stay on needles and pins, anxiously trying to get going.

At the beginning of training a horse to stand quietly under saddle, don't expect him to stand for more than a brief moment at the beginning of a ride. Stop him from moving off of his own accord and then ask him to move in that moment when he *isn't* trying to move. Start the serious training at the end of each ride — first at home and later out on the trail.

When you ask the horse to halt, be sure to be relaxed, letting your weight sink down in the saddle, and your legs rest on his sides. The moment he halts, relax your fingers on the reins without losing contact. That lets him relax so he has a chance to stand still and gives you a chance to tighten the reins by simply closing your fingers each time he tries to move. If you relax the contact by moving your hands forward, he can move a step before you can stop him, and you will startle him by taking contact suddenly. This causes a horse to tense up and move around more.

Check this out — you can have firm contact with your fingers closed and can let the reins droop a full inch in the middle simply by opening your fingers an inch. This is the maximum amount of play you need in the reins when you're first teaching a horse to stand.

You must sit relaxed while you are working on this. If you are tensely waiting for the horse to move, he will. If you are impatiently waiting to continue your ride, the horse will be impatient. It helps if you focus your interest on a leaf or a flower or the clouds while staying fully conscious of the feel of the horse under you. You must sit as if you want to stay there indefinitely but be prepared to stop the horse's movement by closing your fingers. Close one hand slightly before you close the other. This helps keep you from pulling on the reins, which would encourage the horse to pull on the reins and move. Relax your fingers and

Light contact, fingers relaxed — the reins droop slightly.

Firmer contact, fingers closed. My hands haven't moved but the reins are now taut.

Stay relaxed yourself
when you ask a horse to
stand. Pet the horse when
he's standing and being
good, not to quiet him
while he's moving.

repeat the closing until he does stand. The idea is to "talk" him
into it rather than try to force him.

If you are working with a young colt or a nervous horse, you
can't hope to make him stand for more than a brief moment. The
best place to start is at home at the end of a ride where you
normally dismount because he will be more patient there. From
there branch out to other places at home. Dismount when he has
stood still and relaxed. Out on the trail, move him on during a
moment of relaxation and before he tries to move. Do this again
at another place and another, gradually getting him to stand for
longer periods. Pick out places where he can stand comfortably.
You wouldn't stand long with one foot on the bank and the other
in the ditch. Neither will he.

If your way of riding is to keep your horse hyper and to jerk on
the reins for fast stops and turns, you can't hope to teach your
horse to stand quietly. Correct this by getting him to relax and go
forward willingly. If you jerk on the reins or hit the horse to
punish him for not standing, you can't hope for him to relax and
stand. Patiently train him bit-by-bit to stand for longer periods.
Eventually he will learn to stand on a completely loose rein if
you are consistent about getting him to relax and never let him
move off of his own accord at any time.

10

Vices Under Saddle

Biting

Horses that bite and kick other horses when they are being ridden aren't really being ridden — they are being sat upon. Horses naturally bite or kick others when they feel their territory is being invaded or their superior position is being threatened. However, a saddle horse must accept whatever position you put him in. If you are riding a boss-type horse that wants to bite to keep other horses in line, you have to pay more attention so you can train him not to assert himself.

The very first move such a horse makes is to swing his head toward the other horse beside him. This is his way of telling the other horse to stay back where he belongs. This head movement may be very slight, with a brief flattening of the ears. Stay alert for this kind of threat when you're riding beside another horse. Even if your horse is not aggressive, pay close attention because the fact that you are on him may make him feel brave. I have seen this happen more than once. The most notable time was when my husband Bill started riding Dos and I rode with him one day on Pi Dough. Dos was always low man among the horses and Pi Dough was herd boss, but Dos felt safely reinforced with Bill on his back so he flattened his ears and swung his head at Pi Dough.

If your horse is obedient to your legs, all you have to do for a minor swing of your horse's head is to close your legs suddenly and firmly on him as he does it. If your horse is already confirmed in biting at horses beside him, be ready for him to make his move. Ride with contact with his mouth to limit his reach. If he is overly aggressive, slap him on the neck with your hand and speak sharply as you close your legs firmly and suddenly. Get a friend to help you by riding beside you so you can make it a training session. Always stay alert when riding beside any other horses.

When you get it well established in the horse's mind that his aggression always brings punishment, you can remind him by simply closing your legs and wiggling the reins slightly. Don't ride such a horse (or any horse) up on the tail of the horse ahead because he may try to bite that horse's rump and you are not in a good position to reprimand him for it. You aren't just punishing the horse; when you close your legs you are also getting his attention and sending him forward. Pushing him into the heels of the horse ahead could precipitate a battle.

Kicking

This brings us to the kicking problem. Mares are especially good at kicking at other horses, but it is not a totally sex-linked action. Even nonaggressive horses can be pushed into kicking to defend themselves. One often-used excuse that I will not accept is that the mare is coming in heat. More misbehavior in mares is blamed on that one thing than on anything else. If a stallion, who is "in heat" all the time, can be trained to be a gentleman in company,

The aggressive horse is inclined to bite the horse in front of him.

then a mare can certainly be trained to be a lady. It is just a case of training her — or any horse — to be obedient.

Horses almost always give a warning that they will kick. First comes the tense, violent swish-swish side-to-side with the tail. The horse may hit the horse behind with one hard swat with his tail or he may hump up his rear end in a warning kick-motion. If he is really planning to kick, he will slow down, clamp his tail, and gather his hind legs under him. If he suddenly clamps his tail, lowers his haunches, and scoots forward, he won't kick unless the threat from behind keeps up with him. You have a dual responsibility in dealing with the kicking problem: Don't let your horse kick; and don't ride up behind or close beside any horse, especially one that swishes his tail at you.

> Humans, like horses, cannot kick and go forward at the same time.
>
> — Benedict

Benedict was right: Horses can't kick when they're going forward willingly, with energy. Every semester there is at least one kicky horse in each of my classes. It is nerve-racking trying to prevent accidents until I can get these horses going forward willingly with relaxed energy. Once this is established, the horse is no longer in position to try to kick and the rider has instant control if he feels the horse think about kicking.

When your horse swishes his tail side-to-side or up and down, drive him forward with your legs (and the whip, too, if necessary) to keep him going with energy and rhythm. It doesn't make any difference whether he is a kicker or not — he should not be allowed to think about kicking. If your horse is a kicker, don't worry about using your legs at first if that is difficult for you. Just clobber the horse a good one with the whip when he does any of the things that usually lead up to kicking.

Now I'm not telling you that your horse shouldn't swish his tail at all, I'm talking about the times he swishes it at other horses or people or dogs or whatever. If you are very consistent about punishing a kicker whenever he threatens another horse, you will soon be able to control him just by closing your legs firmly each time he even thinks he might want to kick. After you have used the whip hard for two or three offenses, try using just your legs. You can always add a zing with the whip if you need to. If you continue to zap him hard for each offense, he will get so he leaps ahead every time any horse approaches from the rear.

When you zap him with the whip, don't jerk him back with the reins. Let him jump ahead a stride or two and then keep him moving in an energetic trot. If he kicks when you hit him, immediately hit him again. It is best to set up a training program with one other rider for a while so you don't have to contend with horses all around you. One reason horses go on and on misbehaving is because the rider doesn't take time out to work on the cure. Just hoping to catch an occasional disobedience at the right time won't cure the horse. For one thing, you will be too late with the punishment or driving the horse forward. For another, you won't get the training opportunity often enough to replace the bad habit with the good one. Take the time and effort to work consistently on the cure.

Bucking

Horses shouldn't be allowed to buck. The old cowboy saying that a horse isn't worth much if he doesn't buck the first time he's ridden is a bunch of baloney. Maybe most horses will give up bucking if you ride it out the first time, but my experience has proven that they just get better and better at it even if you don't get bucked off. Being able to ride a bucking horse may make you a good rider, but it doesn't prove you are a good trainer. When I start a colt, I take great pains to educate him step-by-step so he won't be likely to buck, and to prevent his bucking if he does try.

But what about the horse that has already learned to buck? Can you prevent it and cure it? Usually you can; and the place to start is to eliminate the causes. I got on one horse in class and had ridden it a couple of times around a large circle in the trot when its owner said, "I forgot to tell you — she bucks." When I was young and rambunctious, I didn't mind the bucking. I even ruined one horse and started to ruin another because I enjoyed it, but now I know better and don't care so much for the rough riding. So when this girl said her horse bucked, I momentarily tensed up and then immediately told myself, "Don't be silly. You aren't going to do anything to make this horse buck."

One big reason a horse bucks is that the rider's hands keep punishing its mouth and the rider keeps giving conflicting aids. The rider kicks the horse so hard it spurts ahead, jerks on the reins to slow it down, suddenly jerks its head around to turn a corner, and then whips or kicks the horse for sticking its head up in the air and taking off. The poor horse finally bucks in complete frustration.

Just changing from a curb bit to a snaffle and changing your slap-dash riding habits for steady, thoughtful ones can cure many horses of wanting to buck. It's the same old story: Use an easy bit and maintain contact so the horse knows at all times where the bit is and the horse will relax. Keep your mind on the feel of the horse underneath you so you use your aids just the amount necessary — and no more — and the horse will relax. Plan ahead for every change of direction and gait so you don't startle the horse and he will relax. A relaxed horse doesn't buck.

The majority of people who write to me about the bucking horse problem have it only when putting the horse into the canter or lope. Their horses are gentle and obedient otherwise. It is easier for a horse to buck from the canter since he is already bounding, but the reason he bucks at this time is because it is natural for a horse to put in a few buck jumps when cantering or because the rider aids him too suddenly and too severely in trying to get the canter.

A lot of people feel they must kick the horse hard to get the canter, and lots of them jerk on the horse's mouth each time they kick him. Many riders try to teach a horse to take a slow canter right from the start and so hold the horse severely with the reins. This makes him put his head up and his back down, which makes it painful and difficult for him to canter. Others think they must make the reins loose to let the horse take the canter, and then they jerk his mouth to slow him down the moment he starts cantering. All of these things can confuse and hurt the horse enough to make him buck when he canters.

Don't canter your bucking horse early in the ride. Stiff muscles or sheer exuberance (especially on a cold, brisk morning) can cause him to buck. Train him to take the canter easily, first from the trot on a large circle and later from the walk. By cantering on a large circle at first, you don't have to try to control the speed — just let the circle do it. You can use a long, gradual slope the same way — let the uphill pull control the speed of the canter. By picking up the canter from the trot, the horse already has more forward motion and can go into the canter more easily.

Always have your horse relaxed before you ask him for the canter. Always maintain contact with his mouth when you ask; otherwise he will just trot faster. If you maintain contact and push him with your legs and seat a little more each stride, he will eventually change to the canter. As you feel him start to make the change, relax your hands a little without losing contact. Push him on in the canter, letting the circle or the hill control his speed.

As the horse gains more experience in changing to the canter and accepts the bit more, he will make the change more easily. This is because he will begin to balance toward the rear and lift himself into the canter instead of losing his balance and falling into it. You can definitely feel this shift in balance. The horse maintains his basic speed in the trot, his forehand gets lighter, and then you can give the little extra push that makes him lift and canter. By training him this way and by preparing him for the canter by pushing him onto the bit, you avoid having to hit or kick him suddenly and thus avoid his making that initial buck jump. Later on (in Chapter 12) I will deal with problems connected with slowing the canter.

Horses that are already in the habit of bucking at the canter may still offer to do so. Any time a horse offers to buck, don't bring him to a stop. If you do that, pretty soon he will buck just to get to stop. Instead, brace your arms against your body and immediately relax them without losing contact. As you do this, lean back and drive the horse forward with your seat and legs. Bracing your arms briefly makes the horse's head go up. Driving him forward makes him quit trying to buck. A horse can't buck when he's going forward with energy. Continue to drive strongly with your seat and legs until he quits trying to buck — *then*

When a horse thinks of bucking, brace your arms briefly to keep his head up, lean back and drive him forward.

control his speed. Usually you shouldn't try to hold the horse's head up because that will slow him down and put him in a position to buck better, but sometimes it is necessary. To raise his head, extend your arms and lift your hands so you are pulling up, not back, on the reins. Maintain contact as you do this.

Any horse that bucks indiscriminately should be taught to double. You don't need to double the horse that just puts in a buck jump or two when you first ask him to canter — just drive him on. But the horse that breaks in two when the notion strikes him can be retrained by booting him into a double the moment he thinks of bucking. If you wait until he is already bucking hard, it is too late and you can throw him down. Get him on that first jump: Double him and boot him out; double him back the other way and boot him forward in a trot. Keep him moving.

Keep in mind that a horse must slow down to buck. When you feel your horse traveling with his emergency brake on, send him forward. Some badly spoiled horses will buck just because you have told them to go forward more. Ride such a horse in a corral with a high fence; boot him out and double him several times and then trot him forward, working for a steady rhythm and relaxation. Every time the horse gets stubborn about going forward, boot him out and double him. When he has learned that he must go forward when you ask, then you can ride him other places and keep him moving, doubling him only as necessary to prevent his bucking.

Backing

Many people have trouble backing a horse because they don't understand the mechanics of it. Many trainers who successfully teach a horse to back, do so through sensitive application of force rather than applying the proper principles. As a result, horses use several defenses against stepping back, the main one being to stand there very firmly. Some will rear or toss their heads and dance around. Some will back a step or two and then whirl around, while others will back okay but not in a straight line.

Because a horse can refuse to back so effectively and because people don't understand the principle involved, some people try things such as having the horse squirted with water or threatened in front with a broom. Others try spurring him on the shoulders or even using a breast collar with tacks in it, thinking the horse will back away from the pain when the rider pulls on the breast collar. An especially cruel variation of this is the use of barbed wire on the breast or nose.

All these problems and weird pseudo-solutions come about because people think a horse should back up from stronger pull on the reins. Study horses running loose. The only time a horse moves his head back first is when another horse threatens him in his face. Then he pulls his head back and drags himself backward. If a horse wants to step back, he does so, and his head follows simply because it's attached. The horse that goes forward

When a horse won't yield to the bit, he won't back freely or won't back at all.

Iam yields and steps back correctly as I close my legs. His ears rotate back more because of the direction of travel.

willingly and yields to the bit will step back when asked to move into a less-yielding rein. By training your horse in the proper order — first to go forward and yield to the bit, then to back — you can eliminate all the bad problems connected with backing.

To back freely, a horse must step back precisely with his legs moving in diagonal pairs. In order to do this, he must relax, shift his balance toward the rear and keep his nose down. He can't relax if you are hurting him with a hard pull on the reins or with some pain-inflicting gadget. He can't balance toward the rear if his head is stuck up in the air or his feet are planted out in front and behind. He won't keep his nose down if he won't yield to the bit (see Chapter 4).

When your horse will go forward willingly and come to a square halt from the walk, staying soft on the bit, you can start asking him to back. Ask him to yield to the bit; then without yielding to him, close your legs on him to ask him to move. Because you don't yield with your hands, he steps to the rear. As he does so, relax your aids and move him forward. Never try to get a horse to back by pulling on the reins. After he will easily back one step, you can gradually get him to back two, then three, etc., by applying and relaxing the aids in rhythm with his steps back.

Horses back crooked because the rider holds the reins unevenly and/or applies his legs unevenly. Make sure you take equal contact with the horse's mouth. If the horse then starts backing off to the left, close your left leg more firmly to move him away from it and vice versa. And remember that a horse must have faith that you will back him into a clear area. If you destroy this trust by backing him into things, he may never back again — at least not for a long while.

11

Shying

Gaining the horse's trust

Horses shy for a variety of reasons. Any horse can be startled by a sudden noise or by the sudden appearance of a person, animal, or thing. At such times remain calm; close your legs firmly and talk to your horse in a matter-of-fact tone of voice, neither scolding nor wheedling. He will be relieved to know that one of you has kept his head.

A horse's basic disposition enters into shying. Some horses are bold from birth while others are born to be cautious. I don't care much for the horse that will plow through anything because he could get me in trouble and besides, he will usually plow through me. Sometimes extreme nervousness can be caused by a nutritional imbalance. If your horse is nervous about everything, try two tablespoons of bone meal and one tablespoon of Epsom salts (magnesium) daily mixed with his grain. It could cure his problem and you can always discontinue it if he doesn't get better in about a month.

Basic shying comes from the horse's inexperience. Young horses and horses that have led sheltered lives will be nervous in new surroundings. Country-raised horses will be afraid of things that town-raised horses think nothing about. Iam wants to go see every tractor he hears running and to investigate all the fascinating things in every yard. Cars and motorcycles are his normal environment, yet a bare patch in the middle of a grassy field or a shallow ditch can be scary to him.

While inexperience doesn't usually deter the naturally bold horse, the naturally suspicious horse will want to proceed with caution. There are times that even the experienced horse will be suspicious of some noise or object and want to stop, look, and listen. If you want to cure a horse of shying, you have to learn to understand his reasons. Is he truly scared and in need of your support and reassurance? Is he using shying as an excuse to get out of work? Maybe he's just feeling exuberant or is bored and wants to liven things up. If you don't read him right, you can do the wrong thing.

Green horses and those that are truly scared of some object shouldn't be hit to try to make them go up to the object or through the scary place. This only convinces the horse that he was right to be scared because the thing is hurting him. Let the horse stop and take a good look. Don't try to move him forward until you feel him relax. If necessary, get off, but don't try to lead him up to the thing. Talk in a matter-of-fact voice to him. This is very important. You must sound as if this is the most ordinary, insignificant thing you have ever seen. As the horse relaxes, you can gradually get him to follow you step-by-step up to the scary rock, black log, bridge, water, or whatever.

Don't ever pet a horse while he is being or acting scared, thinking to calm him down. You are just rewarding him for his fearful actions. Pet him when he makes a definite move in the right direction. When the horse does seem to accept the terrifying "booger," still take the time to hang around nonchalantly and ride around or through it several times. Gradually the horse will learn to trust you in more and varied situations and you won't have to spend so much time educating him.

How can you tell whether a horse is truly scared or just putting you on? It isn't always easy. In the first place you should train your horse at home to go forward willingly. Secondly, you should psych yourself out to remain relaxed at all times. When you approach that same rock he was so scared of yesterday, stay relaxed. If he starts to show signs of being scared — pricking his ears, raising his head, and tensing his muscles — tell him in a conversational way, "It's just that same old rock." Immediately look straight ahead — not at the rock — and rhythmically use your legs to keep him moving on. Use this same technique on new spooks, too. If he trusts you he may detour a little; but he will keep going even if he does it cautiously.

If he trusts you . . . This is one big key to this shying business. Any young horse or horse that's new to you and his surroundings will probably be apprehensive. If you build his trust in you as you work with him, he will become more and more agreeable about taking your word for the safety of the situation. You build a horse's trust by what you ask of him and how you ask it, by being consistent, by praising him for good work however small, and by keeping cool when things go wrong. If you ask a young horse to negotiate rough terrain or get tough with your horse to make him plow through a scary situation, he will feel that you aren't to be trusted. If you go along ignoring his little disobediences and then suddenly explode over them, or blame him for disobeying when actually he just doesn't understand, you can't build his trust in you. If you learn to think like a horse and treat him accordingly, he will learn to trust your judgment.

The nervous rider

If you are nervous about anything while working around the horse, he will be nervous. You may be uptight wondering if he is going to buck today; he will spot a black log ahead and think he'd better get uptight about that. By being tense, you can teach a horse to shy. When we first moved our horses to rattlesnake country, all seven of them couldn't have cared less if a snake buzzed under their feet. I was the one who was apprehensive, tensing up excitedly over every encounter. It wasn't long before my saddle horses learned to leap away from a buzzing rattler. It doesn't pay to act nervous around horses — it makes them think there may be something they should be nervous about.

When Iam hasn't been ridden for a while and we're moving along the trail at a vigorous trot, he often uses a log or stump for an excuse to leap sideways and then try for a few buck jumps. This is just the joy of getting out for a ride. When I ride him in the arena, he will start out working fine; but after about fifteen minutes, he will suddenly decide he should steer clear of the letters around the outside, certain bushes, and all bird chirps. This is a sign he is bored because I didn't vary the warming-up exercises enough. In the first case I just keep him moving until the edge is off. In the second, I firmly tell him with legs and voice he has to keep working. If I remember to add variety to his work, I have no trouble with his shying in the arena.

Going through water

When my editor came up to take photos of me and Iam for this book, we hauled him to a place he had never been before. I was hoping to get examples of a horse balking at water and shying, but he has had three years of training and learning to trust me. I had to stop him at the water's edge because he was going to walk right into the strange stream — a proof that my training methods are sound. It did puzzle me that he didn't shy at anything until I happened to think — he's in a strange place, he trusts me, and he's too interested in everything to be apprehensive.

I will tell you how I trained Iam to go through water. This will show you how to handle that and similar situations, and how to tell when the horse is no longer scared but is just using shying against you.

Lots of folks say Arabs are naturally scared of water but I don't believe it. I have gathered lots of data on the subject and am sure that lack of experience has far more to do with it than the desert breeding of their ancient ancestors. Iam was inexperienced. When I was ponying him before he was old enough to ride, I stopped at the edge of the streams when he did. Then I rode Pi Dough just barely into the water and waited. Iam would sniff and

Sharyn plays in the puddle to show Smoki it can be fun.

Smoki wants to smell and feel, so Sharyn accommodates him, but keeps a good hold on the reins in case he should decide to bolt.

snort and finally take a cautious step or two. Then I could lead him on in, but I always had difficulty getting him out because he found it so much fun. Pi Dough had shown him it was safe to get his feet wet.

When I started riding him, he no longer had Pi Dough's support, and he didn't yet trust my judgment on the safety of the footing. Even though he had learned to be led into the water without hesitation, being ridden in was an entirely new experience to him. I avoided stream banks because even a slight drop-off into water presents double jeopardy to a horse. Iam balked and I just sat there with each hand out to the side to keep him from turning either way. When he wanted to put his head down to smell and feel, I let him, gathering the reins up as his head came up so I remained in control. Each time I felt him relax, I closed my legs to ask him to step forward; each time he tensed up, I just sat there. When he finally went in, I let him nose all around in the water to satisfy his curiosity. If he had started pawing, I would have moved him on vigorously to keep him from lying down. Water should be pleasant for the horse, but not that pleasant!

When I hauled Iam out to Whiskeytown for hill climbing and a variety of trail experiences, I chose the water crossings in the order of their difficulty. The first two were no trouble because they were flat road crossings. The third one still had a gradual entry, but it was steeper. Iam flatly refused this one, so that called for plan number two. If a horse is scared, he can overcome his fear a lot by seeing another horse go first. If you use another horse, he should be stopped in the water out of the way instead of just ridden across. The best principle is to show the scared horse that it is safe, not to take advantage of his not wanting to be left behind. Be sure your lead horse will go on through anything.

When you are riding alone, as I was, you have to be the other horse. Even a colt that doesn't fully trust you yet will decide it is safe to go on if you go first and don't try to force him to follow. The water here was deeper, but off to the side was a large rock with about a square foot of dome rising above the water. Right here I made a mistake. Rather than fill my boots with water, I waded out to the rock and stood on it, talking conversationally to Iam. He soon wanted to follow me, but he couldn't because the rock wasn't big enough for both of us. After all, his reasoning was that the safe place to walk was where I walked. I finally did get him to cross by getting out of his way, but it took several crossings later before he would go straight on without trying to detour to step on that rock.

The next ride or so out, I took an alternate route to include a different crossing. Iam had to learn to cross where and when I told him, not just at certain places. This place was flat and should have been easy, but the sand on either side was wet and darker than the road. To Iam a change in color of the footing was

Get your feet wet to show the horse it's safe. Using the stepping stones could invite the horse to do the same.

spookier than the water, so, back in the water again for me. Plan 2B — don't just wade in and wait. Get in there and play in the water, splashing it discreetly with your foot and generally having horse-type fun (you don't have to lie down and roll) while you ignore the horse. After a while he will decide that he wants part of the action. Then lead him across a few times and ride him back and forth a few times before continuing your ride. Lots of petting and praising is in order, but only when he comes forward, not when he is balking.

Incidentally, I always wear my new boots and go early in the morning for water training. If you have to wade in, keep your boots on the rest of the day until they dry. It's the best way there is to break in new boots. You can rub in lots of oil or b'ar grease after they dry.

I saved the fifth water crossing for last because the water is a little swift there and even experienced horses have trouble finding places in it to put their feet between the scattered boulders. The approach, although fairly flat, winds narrowly through clumps of boulders. Maybe I was expecting Iam to balk. Maybe it was just the trouble I was having finding footing myself. At any rate, Iam wasn't about to follow me in. Checking him out, I could see that his eyes were soft and his muscles were relaxed. He showed no sign of apprehension, but he must have been enjoying the spectacle of his rider stumbling around over the rocks in that stream.

I simply mounted him, took down my quirt, and told him with one good swat to go on across. The time had come when he was no longer afraid of the water but would use it as an excuse to get out of work. There is really no way I can tell you how to know the difference except to check for signs in the horse's eyes, his muscles, and his way of standing — poised for flight or simply stuck in the ground. If you have been careful to make his initial experiences good ones, it is much easier to tell when he has decided balking is a fun game.

To sum all this up, work to gain your horse's trust and his obedience to go forward willingly. Stay relaxed and matter-of-fact. Don't pet a horse for shying but don't punish him either by trying to whip him up to the thing he is scared of. Use two

Use two leading reins on contact to keep the horse from turning away. Don't pet him for refusals, thinking that it will calm him.

When the horse relaxes, move him forward. Now praise him and pet him.

leading reins to keep him from turning away, and ask him to move forward only when he relaxes. Go first to show him it is safe but don't try to force him to lead on. These things apply to bridges, boulders, water, black logs — anything that spooks a horse. When you see that the horse is no longer scared, don't hesitate to be firm and sudden in moving him on.

Even older, trained horses will often want to shy away from many of these objects alongside the trail. I agree that horses have astigmatism. I have it and I know that it is a case of identification. If a thing doesn't move, I can mistake it for any number of things. When a thing moves (except unexpectedly out from under his feet) the horse is usually able to identify it and relax. Until it moves, he isn't sure it doesn't present a danger to him.

Turning a horse's head toward a fearsome object allows him to shy out and around it.

With his head turned away and his haunches held straight by my left leg, which is moved back, Iam walks on past the "booger" without shying.

Going straight past a "booger"

When a horse is responsive to your legs, going forward when the leg is closed at the cinch and keeping his haunches straight when the leg is closed a little farther back, you can safely control him going past these things he has trouble identifying. Suppose you are riding along the road and your horse shows fear of a boulder ahead on your right. Most people will try to get the horse past this spook by keeping his head pointed toward it. The horse then makes a sidepassing detour around the thing, ending up on the far side still facing it. Then he gets to turn away thus figuring he finally escaped. During all of this the horse is actually out of control.

The proper way to handle this situation on the trained horse (and response to your legs should be part of his earliest training) is to turn his head slightly away from that boulder on your right. At the same time keep him moving forward with your left leg at the cinch and keep him from whirling away by moving your right leg back to keep his haunches straight. If you have to reinforce your driving aid with the whip, use it on the left side. The horse may sidle a little away from the boulder, but he will go on past it under your control. None of this business of making a wide semi-circle facing the spook. Reverse the aids, of course, if the "booger" is on your left.

Training for traffic

A horse should not be ridden in traffic until he has been educated to it. I don't care for it even then. It's bad enough to drive in it when you're in a car, surrounded by steel armor and still having to watch in all directions for all the other fools on the road. A horse doesn't give you much protection and he can become frightened and run right into danger.

The way to train a horse to accept all sorts of vehicles is to ride him behind them as they go away from him. As long as he is "chasing" them, he doesn't feel threatened and his natural curiosity will even help him stay relaxed and moving. You should keep him moving at first. After he is used to various vehicles, he can be asked to stand and watch them go by. When he has

Take advantage of the horse's natural boldness in chasing fleeing vehicles to train him to relax in traffic.

learned to accept their motion and noise, he can accept them better when they come up behind him and at him.

The best place to do this training is in an open field near a road. There you have room to get closer to the traffic gradually and to maneuver so you can chase the cars instead of being chased. If you don't have such a field available, get the help of your folks or friends to drive cars and motorcycles under controlled conditions for you. After your horse is used to motorcycles, don't expect him to automatically accept bicycles. They don't make noise and so are a special kind of monster to him.

Incidental ''boogers''

Another thing that can scare a horse, making you think he has flipped, is a person standing or sitting still and not saying a word. Again it's his astigmatism at work. Get the person to start talking and to move a little. Then there's the tree or bush that suddenly becomes two instead of one. One time I was out on Dos with my black shepherd, who was making the usual canine circles to cover as much territory as possible. Ahead, a few feet from the trail, was a black stump which Dos paid no attention to. (Dos doesn't shy at anything.) As we neared the stump, it split into a black stump and a black dog, and Dos decided it was time to split. A silent person stepping away from a tree will affect a horse the same way.

There are some things that will startle any horse — birds or rabbits suddenly bursting into motion out from under their feet, noises in the brush or around the corner whose source they can't identify, and rocks they kick up that go rolling ahead of them. In most cases the answer is to quietly and firmly keep the horse moving forward. If he is obviously panicky, you may have to keep him on a circle for a while until he can start thinking again. If, however, the thing startles him from behind so he bolts ahead, the answer is to sink your weight down and brace your arms to firmly drive him onto the bit to stop him, then to immediately move him on under control. If the horse is green, double him and keep him moving.

Dogs can present a dangerous problem. The worst ones are the silent heelers. I always keep a lookout for dogs. If they are troublesome, I turn my horse and herd them around for a while. This teaches the horse that he is superior to dogs and doesn't have to fear them. Letting your own dog go along on rides is a good way to get a colt over being startled easily, if you are experienced enough to control the colt through moving him and doubling when necessary.

In all cases of shying, stay calm and keep thinking. Remember that the horse is depending upon your reaction to determine his own.

12

Leads

The questions I have received on leads range from "What are they?" to "How do I get a flying change?" Some people have written that they can't get their horses to canter. Almost all horses love to canter — in fact some of them love to do it much faster than we would like — so the whole thing is a matter of getting the canter (and leads) when we ask, not just when the horse feels like it.

We speak of leads only in relation to the canter or gallop. In this gait the horse reaches farther forward with both the front and hind legs on one side — the left legs in the left lead and the right legs in the right lead. I feel that everyone should learn to get either lead from his horse, simply for the experience of being able to get command performance.

More importantly, a horse can't turn well to the right when loping on the left lead and vice versa. He could even fall in a short turn, so it is best for you to be able at least to tell which lead your horse is on so you can first ask for the trot before you turn if your horse isn't up to flying changes. You should be able to tell by feel which lead your horse is on, and the way to learn this feel is to look first and then feel. Even though it makes it more difficult for the horse to lope when you lean forward, do take a quick look over his shoulder to see which forefoot is leading (reaching farther forward). Then sit back and feel how the horse puts that side of you farther forward. Soon you will be able to feel without looking.

There is another feel you should know about even though your horse may not give you the opportunity to experience it — that

This horse is on the wrong lead and having difficulty making the turn.

of the horse's going disunited. The horse is disunited when he canters on one lead in front and the other one behind. There are two kinds of bumpy feelings in the canter. One is from riding with a stiff back and hanging on with your legs or pushing your feet hard on the stirrups. This causes you to be thrown off the horse's back in the direction of travel. The other bumpiness is from the horse's being disunited, and it bumps your seatbones in a sort of syncopated beat that gives them a hula twist.

Laying the foundation for leads

There isn't any shortcut to training a horse to take his leads on command. The proper foundation must be laid; and if you are having problems with a one-lead horse, it will take a long time and much patience to lay that foundation. If you try to go on with showing your horse or entering him in games during this training, you may never get him to take his leads consistently. Haste in this matter will waste all your efforts.

The proper foundation is to get your horse to travel straight on a circle. That means he will bend his spine full length to match the arc of the circle. To get this, you must sit up straight on your horse and look where you are going. Turn slightly in the waist as you move your inside hand only about an inch in the direction of your outside shoulder. This combination lengthens the outside rein and holds the horse's inside shoulder in place as it flexes his head barely in the direction of the circle or turn. At the same time you must put your outside leg back to keep his haunches from drifting out and you must drive with your inside leg to bend his body out and keep him moving in rhythm.

In getting the canter from the trot initially, you simply urge the horse forward a little more each stride without softening the contact on his mouth until he eventually goes into the canter. If you lessen the contact on his mouth (thinking to free him so he can canter), he will just trot faster. Your hands should go with his head motion *after* he takes the canter, not before. So ride a large circle until the horse is traveling relaxed and rhythmic in the trot, bent to the arc of the circle. Then simply push him gradually into the canter without changing his bend or getting him excited. He will take the proper lead almost every time.

If the horse doesn't take the proper lead — left lead going counterclockwise and vice versa — it is because he wasn't bent properly at the moment he changed to the canter. Dos was very clever at this. He could unbend and canter in the twinkling of an eye and was so smooth on the wrong lead that I would have to look to make sure. Feel the lead without looking if you possibly can but do look if necessary. It won't hurt anything for the horse to canter on the wrong lead for a few strides while you make sure.

Never punish a horse in any way for taking the wrong lead. Quietly bring him back to the trot, reestablish the relaxed, rhythmic trot with the proper bend, and try again. Make sure you don't yield with the reins until the horse lifts into the canter because that would give him a chance to unbend. Don't try to bend him with the inside rein. That would bend his neck only and would shorten his stride. Drive with your inside leg because this pushes the middle of his body out in the proper bend and causes him to stride farther forward with his inside hind leg. Your outside leg behind the girth should merely keep his haunches from drifting out.

A horse that has been punished, intentionally or otherwise, for taking the wrong lead can be almost impossible to retrain. Daniel came to me after being worked on by others and given up as impossible. He wouldn't accept equal contact or keep his head straight and wouldn't bend to the rider's legs. There is no way to control such a horse to get a designated lead, so I put him on the longe to teach him the basics. When he was bending, accepting the bit, and trotting relaxed, I began asking for the canter and could get his lead to the right (the bad side) 97 percent of the time on the longe.

When I felt that Daniel was far enough along on the longe, I tried him under saddle. He was beginning to bend to the circle and accept the bit, but the moment I tried to push him quietly into a canter going to the right, he would get frantic, throw his head up, and take the left lead. This was because he had been hassled so much by people who tried to force him to take that lead. Even though we eventually made enough progress that Daniel would occasionally take the right lead under saddle, it would take a long time to overcome the psychological damage and to train his rider to make him consistent. He's an excellent trail horse and should be used on trails, not in shows and gymkhanas. The money spent in retraining him would buy a good show-games horse.

Because the horse's left foreleg reaches farther forward in going on the left lead, many people mistakenly suppose he stretches the left side of his body. This leads to the mistaken theory that you should free the horse's left side so he can take his left lead. Actually, because he also reaches farther forward with his left hind leg in the left lead, he must compensate by contracting his

Trying to bend a horse with the inside rein bends only his neck and shortens his stride.

body on the left side. When a relaxed horse moves his left hind leg forward in any gait, his body always swings to the right. Therefore, bending the horse correctly for going on a circle to the left will make it easy for him to take the left lead. All systems are reversed for the right lead.

When you keep the horse bent properly along the arc of the large circle while pushing him into the canter, you aren't training him to take his leads; you are putting him in the position where he will take them naturally. When you push him gradually into the canter, you are getting him to make the change simply because he can't maintain his balance any longer in the trot. When these things are becoming easy for you and your horse, begin working toward precise performance by consistently using all the right aids, first in the simple situation on the large circle, next in riding through corners, and finally in going straight.

In order to lift into the canter instead of just "falling" into it, the horse must develop strength and must shift his balance toward the rear. Even when he is well balanced in all his work, the horse must momentarily balance back a little more in order to lift into a canter. You get him to do this by pushing him forward onto your unyielding hands. This is called a *half-halt*. Relax your hands in one stride or less because it is just a short push onto a briefly unyielding bit, to put the horse together.

Putting together all that I've just explained about leads, the following are the proper aids for asking for the left lead on the circle, through the corner, and going straight. There are plenty of other aids expounded for this, but only the following aids will get a horse to make a gallop depart on the designated lead while staying straight on the track. This isn't just for looks, it is also for better control of your horse with less effort.

Bend your horse to the left. If you are on the circle or going through a corner, you should already have him bent. Going straight, bend him as if you were on a very large circle to the left. Half-halt on the right (outside) rein only. You do this by fixing your right hand as you drive with your left (inside) leg. You should feel the horse get lighter and his trot get more energetic, as if he really wants to move, but he shouldn't go any faster. If he doesn't feel this way, half-halt again on the right rein in the next

The change (transition) from trot to canter on the left lead. The horse's balance is to the rear. The rider had leaned forward, dropped contact, and over-aided, causing the horse's head to come up.

stride. Aid him into the canter with another push with your left leg. Ride the canter as he canters on.

These aids are just the ones needed to bend the horse on the circle, plus the half-halt on the outside rein and the push with the inside leg. If you use these aids consistently, developing the horse's ability and understanding first on the circle, then through the corners, and finally going straight, you should have no trouble with leads. Relax so you apply your aids in rhythm with the horse's strides. Never bend the horse with the inside rein alone —

Shirley and Misty go through a canter corner correctly: The rider is positioned properly and the horse is bent to the corner and striding under.

The author practicing
riding the canter in the
round corral. Note how
far under Iam strides with
his hind leg.

make sure you always drive him onto the outside rein with your
inside leg and put your outside leg back to hold his haunches. If
you have trouble when going straight, go back to the circle and
corners to get the canter aids more firmly established.

One reason people have so much trouble with leads is that
they expect to have trouble. This makes the rider tense, and
tension makes the rider stiffen and get out of balance with the
horse. This can create such a problem that it makes it difficult just
to get the horse to take the canter, period. If you have this basic
problem, practice relaxing and riding the canter (without making
sharp turns) before you start worrying about leads.

The best place for this is in the 60-foot round corral where you
can practically turn your horse loose while you practice, thus
avoiding interfering with his canter. A long, very gradual slope is
a safe place to boot your horse into a canter and give him his
head while you practice. A fenced lot about 100 feet each way
will work. Let your weight sink down into the saddle; relax your
waist so your seat can follow the horse's back; let the horse
position you on his back as you sit up straight and look where
you are going. Cantering can be lots of fun for both of you.
Control the horse enough so that he doesn't run but don't worry
about trying for a slow canter. You must be relaxed to aid a horse
for leads.

Most horses have a preference for one lead, usually the left
one. Although almost all problems with leads are developed by

some rider somewhere along the line, there are some cases when a horse can't or won't take a certain lead. If you have a one-sided horse, watch him running loose to see if he always takes the same lead. If so, he probably has an unsoundness. He also has physical problems if he travels disunited a lot. If he never makes flying changes when he changes direction, you will have trouble teaching him this.

Flying changes

I think the biggest reason people develop so many problems in horses is because they want instant training methods and want to put the frosting on the top before they bake the cake. To get top performance you must patiently follow the whole recipe. So, if you are having problems with leads, go back to the beginning and retrain the horse, first to travel relaxed and rhythmic and to keep the proper bend on the circle. Then you can hope to get the proper lead on the circle, using his natural inclination there to teach him the aids so he will understand and take the lead you ask for anywhere. There isn't any "add-water" package deal that will give you instant success in the matter of leads.

The flying change of leads means that the horse changes from one lead to the other while he is still cantering. The worst mistake you can make in asking for the flying change is to turn the horse suddenly to the opposite side in hopes he will change leads in order to catch himself from falling. If his balance has shifted to his forehand and you compound this by leaning forward, the horse will have difficulty getting the new leading foreleg out from under his body and he could even fall and break a leg. I saw a fellow get a broken leg when his horse fell in just these circumstances.

When a horse will reliably take the designated lead going straight and is balanced to the rear enough that you can easily get a nice canter from the walk, you can start work on the flying change. It is simply a case of putting in a few walk strides between the change of lead, to have time to reverse the bend of the horse. As you and the horse become adept at reversing the bend, gradually decrease the number of walk strides until the horse's understanding and ability have developed to the point where you can ask for the change without coming down from the canter. Reverse your aids for the change on the second or third beat of the canter so the horse has time to change his bend and lead. It is essential that you use all the aids for the proper leads consistently. It is also essential that you get the horse balanced with enough energy coming from the rear so he can make the change.

Slowing the gaits

Getting the horse balanced back and slowing the gallop to a canter (or the lope to a slow lope) and slowing the trot to the jog are all from the same cutting of hay. Any time you pull back on the reins you shorten the stride of the horse's hind legs. Since a horse must get his hind legs forward under him in order to support more weight in the rear, slowing his lope or trot by pulling on the reins just makes him keep his weight on the forehand. The results are stiff, flat gaits that make the horse dink along like an unjointed doll. Western judges no longer want this kind of performance.

You can't force a horse into the jog or slow lope. You must get these gradually by keeping the horse's relaxed energy coming from behind while you gradually get him to accept more shortening of the reins. Then he will learn to perform these gaits with *impulsion* — a soft springing upward. He will also be balanced

Slowing the trot by pulling on the reins leaves the horse strung out and sloppy.

toward the rear — the one thing that makes all good performance possible.

Trying to slow or collect a horse's gaits by pulling on the reins causes several problems. It is the main cause of a high head and headtossing, besides rough hands. It makes some horses canter in either bucking-type leaps or rearing ones. It makes some horses just plain break back to the trot or walk. Never take on the reins without a corresponding push with your legs or pelvis. Never maintain a steady tightening of the reins. All aids must be in rhythm and balanced with each other according to what you want of the horse.

Some horses rush forward in the canter with quick, choppy strides. Some cut through corners, making you feel they may fall at any moment. Some break to the trot in corners. The solution to all three of these situations is to push the horse into longer strides. As the horse's back takes your seat forward, push your whole pelvis farther forward than the horse's back takes it, driving with your inside leg at the same time. Maintain contact on the outside rein. Don't try to turn the horse with your inside rein.

If your horse takes his leads all right when he is running loose but sometimes canters disunited when he is ridden, check up on yourself. You are probably tense and sitting at cross purposes with the horse. Relax. Let the horse position your inside seatbone a little farther forward on the leading side. Keep your shoulders

Pushing the horse onto the bit to slow him puts him together to develop a better jog trot.

When the horse "falls" through a canter corner like this, push him into longer strides and bend the horse with your inside leg.

square, not lined up with your hips. Drive with your inside leg each time your seat goes forward.

If your horse makes his flying change in front first, then goes disunited for a stride or two before changing behind, he isn't balanced to the rear enough and you aren't driving enough with your new leading leg as you ask for the change. Push him into bounding strides and make your aids more definite.

Just remember, there's no magic wand to give you the proper leads. Keep the little part-Arab, Salue, in mind. Her owner was using her in barrel-racing and this handy little horse desperately wanted to go on the proper leads for the turns. She just couldn't do it until her owner learned to sit down in harmony with Salue's movements. Rider interference is the biggest problem horses have with leads.

13

Problems When Mounted

Neckreining

Neckreining shouldn't cause you any problems if you stop thinking of it as that and start thinking of reining the whole horse. You don't have to train a horse to neckrein — he will just naturally learn it if your other training is correct. When Iam was still very green, I was riding him out on the trail and came to a short drop-off into a stream bed. To his inexperienced eye it looked like a drop-off into a canyon. Knowing he was a corral-raised horse and knowing he was still not strong enough to negotiate the bank easily, I automatically reined him to the left toward an easier access.

As we rode on, I thought back to what I had done. On a light rein I had indicated to him through my mind, my legs, and a slight movement of my hand the direction I wanted him to take. Even though he was so green that I had never made the slightest effort to add the touch of the rein to his neck, he responded perfectly to it. He was obedient to my legs and the outside rein, so he "neckreined." This is the secret of putting a good rein on a horse — making him obedient to all the aids.

There are many mistaken ideas about neckreining. Number one on the list is the idea that the horse learns to turn because he feels the rein against his neck. This leads to practices that range from the ludicrous to the barbaric. Those who misunderstand neckreining recommend such things as tapping the horse on the neck with a bat or spurring him in the shoulder to make him turn. They use devices that include tailhair mecates for hackamore reins and tacks in the reins. (Even battery-operated shocking reins were on the market for a while.)

Using pressure of the rein in the middle of this mare's neck causes her to bend in front of the withers and tilt her nose to the outside — as Shirley here demonstrates on Misty.

Thinking that the horse turns from the feel of the rein against his neck leads to using the rein up in the middle of his neck and trying to force him to turn by applying more pressure. This makes the rider sit crooked on the horse; and, when he's using a loose rein, makes him get out of balance by moving his hand farther across the middle of the horse's neck. It also makes the horse tilt his nose to the outside, bend his neck at the withers, and lead with his inside shoulder.

It is true that a trained horse seemingly turns by the touch of the rein only. This is because the horse has been taught one way or another to respond to his rider's body language. The problems people have in neckreining come from not understanding this — from thinking their horses won't learn to neckrein when in reality they haven't been taught to turn. The way to cure these problems is to go back to the beginning and replace bad habits with good ones.

There are a couple of things to keep in mind. One is that you can't control a green or disobedient horse by neckreining. He can bend his neck, as mentioned, or stiffen it like a brick wall — and, in either case, go wherever he pleases. The other thing to remember is that the horse will just naturally neckrein if all your other training is correct. The horse doesn't turn because you neck-reined. He turns because he's obedient to all your aids.

Another demonstration of a poor practice when riding the neckreining horse on a loose rein. Use a longer rein so your elbow stays by your side and your neckreining is just in front of the horse's withers.

After I had ridden Iam in the hackamore for several weeks, I was doing some arena riding with him so I used the snaffle there. Habits are funny things. I learned to use leg aids while learning to use the snaffle, but most of my hackamore riding was before that time. Even though Iam learned to turn quite obediently in the snaffle, there were times then when I rode him in the hackamore that he refused to turn. I discovered I was reverting to my old hackamore habits — forgetting that I have legs. As soon as I remembered to put my outside leg back, he turned easily.

This doesn't mean that you have no use for reins in getting good performance. In order to perform well on light contact a horse must be well balanced toward the rear. To get him balanced you must develop more energy in him. Without the reins to set tactful limits on the rate of movement and direction, the horse would use this energy to just go faster in the direction he prefers.

To teach your horse to neckrein you will have to use an ordinary snaffle bit. A curb bit should never be used until the horse is fully trained. The snaffle gives you independent control of each side of the horse. When you apply one side of the curb bit, you have applied the other side simultaneously. A curb bit with a broken mouthpiece isn't any good because it exerts extreme pressure on the bars of the horse's mouth and it is loose and floppy, which annoys the horse.

To start teaching the horse to neckrein, sit squarely on the horse and keep your hands in the vicinity of his withers. Ride with a rein in each hand until the horse is turning consistently well. When you start riding with both reins in one hand, continue to sit squarely on the horse. Keep your reining hand in front of you and over the horse's withers, never moving it more than an inch to either side independently of your body when riding with a contact.

Train your horse to turn, using all the aids (including inside leg at the girth, outside leg back) so you bend him around the corners the way I described in preparing a horse to take his leads (see p. 124). When he is doing this well, you can begin preparing him for being ridden with one hand. Make use of a fence, a wall, or some solid brush to help the horse turn in his own mind and to shift his balance to the rear. Early in his training start turning him toward the barrier for a smooth half-circle of about 30 feet in diameter. Gradually make the half-circle smaller as his training progresses.

As the circle gets smaller, your outside hand will cross over the withers a little bit as you turn more in the waist to look where you are going. Help balance the horse by moving your outside hand back slightly as you drive more with your inside leg. Whenever the horse doesn't turn well, avoid the temptation to

Using the leading rein as well as my legs to help Iam respond to neckreining. Note the horse's correct bend.

Back view of the leading rein as I help Iam through a wide, neckreining turn.

Shirley and Misty in a very good turn. Misty, who is well trained, responds beautifully as Shirley neckreins properly.

use the reins harder. Use a leading rein to the inside to avoid pulling back on it. The horse doesn't turn well because he has lost his balance — he has fallen onto his forehand. If you pull back on that inside rein, he can't get his inside hind leg under himself to support his weight. If you don't drive him with your inside leg, he loses the energy needed to carry him through the turn.

When the horse is doing so well that you seldom need to use the leading rein inside, take both reins in one hand crossed. This way you can remind him with a turn of the wrist that tightens the inside rein a little bit. This doesn't pull on it, but just serves as a reminder when needed. When he no longer needs this, you can hold the reins coming together in the same direction in your hand. When he reins well this way and is performing well in everything else, he's ready to get acquainted with the curb bit.

Your half-circles (180° turns) should be made in the open as well as against a barrier. The barrier is an aid in his early training. It can help, too, as your horse's training progresses, to turn the half-circles into the pivot. Keep in mind that you never turn a horse for a pivot with the inside rein. You are swinging the whole horse in the turn, not just his head. Your outside leg must be back to hold his haunches in place. The horse must balance back; he must turn on his haunches, not in the middle; and he must bend just a little in the direction of the turn. He can learn to turn right back on himself in the walk and then in the canter for the rollback. He can learn to turn right back from the halt for the pivot. These more advanced turns come about when you consistently use all the aids to balance him back and turn him.

Any time you think of neckreining as moving your hand forward and bringing the rein against the horse's neck, your horse will turn badly. For shorter turns, always move your reining hand back slightly as you drive the horse forward. Always put your outside leg back. Without these things the horse will simply turn on his center in a very poor turn.

On TV recently I watched the finalists in the snaffle bit futurity. Three of those horses pivoted on the center instead of on their haunches. Their riders' feet were shoved forward so there was no control over the horses' haunches. The horses weren't balanced to the rear. They turned by the rein only. To overcome your problems with neckreining, you have to correct your habits so you can control the whole horse. You have to train the horse to turn obediently first — then the neckreining will come naturally and correctly.

The switchtail

Among the miscellaneous problems people have written to me about is the switchtail. A horse will switch his tail to help him keep his balance. In dressage at the Grand Prix level, horses are asked to perform the *piaffe* — the trot in place. These horses switch their tails rhythmically because of the difficulty of maintaining their balance trotting while not moving forward. The rider must develop a great deal of energy in the horse in order to keep him trotting while telling him in essence to stop, therefore

Tyke switches his tail
when his rider overspurs
him to ask for the canter.
Habitual overspurring is
one cause of the habitual
switchtail.

you will often see an extra swish of the tail that means a spur has
been firmly applied.

There is a difference between tail movement to maintain balance and tail-switching. Sudden or excessive application of the
spur can cause tail-switching as well as sudden loss of balance.
Another cause can be pain somewhere. One horse in class that
seemed to have a good disposition was constantly twitching her
tail during work. She also kept her ears pinned back and refused
to keep trotting after being worked for 10 or 15 minutes. Worming didn't help her, but the vet subsequently found some calcium
deposits that were causing her pain. If you think your horse is
ornery and some consistent work doesn't help, start looking for
some physical reason.

Some horses develop the habit of switching or even wringing
their tails constantly while they're working. This gets started
through keeping a horse tense in his training; asking him for
short, quick turns before he is capable; and spurring him to force
him to do the work. You can avoid this bad habit by getting the
horse to go forward in a relaxed and rhythmic manner. Start with
easy turns and build up to the more difficult ones as the horse
becomes more obedient, stronger, and better balanced.

I have never had to try to cure a confirmed switchtail. If I had to try, I would go back to the beginning to get the horse going forward rhythmically with relaxed energy. I would retrain him in logical order to avoid getting him uptight and struggling to keep his balance. It would take time but I feel sure I could succeed.

Using spurs

Avoid using spurs until the horse is far enough along in training to understand what you are asking. They should be used to improve his educated performance, not to force his education. In spurring the horse always lay the side of the spur on his side and roll it upward. Never jab it straight in, no matter what sort of spurs you use.

Mouth problems

I have had many inquiries relating to things a horse does with his mouth. Many people worry about foam, some even thinking it looks horrible. To a knowledgeable horseman, foam is a cause for joy. In order to work well a horse must be relaxed. Think about your own experiences. When you're nervous, your mouth is dry; when you're relaxed, the saliva flows. A moist mouth in a horse indicates that he has relaxed his jaw and accepted the bit. Foam indicates that he is also working with relaxed energy. Some

Regardless of the type of spurs, never jab the horse. Use the side of the rowel or knob and a massaging-upward motion.

horses foam more than others, the work and relaxation being equal, simply because some horses have a greater saliva flow. But a dry mouth in a horse means things aren't going too well.

Some horses insist on putting their tongues over the bit. This is more likely to happen with young horses that are just starting in training. Try adjusting the bit a little higher in the horse's mouth. If that doesn't cure the problem, try a straight-bar snaffle. Use it just long enough to get the horse used to keeping his tongue in place. I started one colt that could pull his tongue out from under any snaffle I put on him. I put my spade bit on him and let him wear it for an hour or two daily in the corral until he no longer fidgeted with the bit. Since he couldn't get his tongue over that mouthpiece, he learned to accept wearing the bit. He then accepted the snaffle so I could ride him.

The horse of any age that opens his mouth when you pull on the reins to ask him to slow down, turn, or stop needs some basic training. His rider needs retraining. The horse is opening his mouth because the rider is pulling. Learn to use your legs and seat to push the horse onto the bit to get him to slow down, turn, and stop. Don't try for fast work before he is responding easily, first in the walk, then the trot, and finally the canter.

Some inquiries have come in about horses that chew or chomp on the bit, others concerning horses grabbing the shank of the curb bit in their mouths. These are all nervous habits developed in various related ways. A nervous horse whose rider doesn't know how to relax him or keeps him hyper, thinking it makes him work better, can develop these bad habits. Using a curb bit to control such a horse can produce the same results. Trying to get fast work through quick, jerky aids or just plain riding with unsteady hands that jerk the horse's mouth can make him very nervous and prone to these mouth habits. An unstable bit such as the so-called western snaffle with the broken mouthpiece also annoys a horse.

In all of these mouth problems the dropped noseband can help because it stabilizes the bit in the horse's mouth and takes some of the pressure off the horse's bars. Use it only with the ordinary snaffle — the bit you should use anyway. The dropped noseband doesn't keep a horse from getting his tongue over the bit or

A properly adjusted dropped noseband stabilizes the bit and transfers some of its pressure to the horse's nose.

opening his mouth. When it is properly adjusted, the horse should be able to take a piece of carrot and eat it easily. You should be able to get two fingers side-by-side under the chin strap.

The cure for these problems is to correct the causes.

There is one kind of chewing on the bit that is desirable. When a horse is relaxed and working well with a relaxed jaw, he often will work his tongue under the bit in a soft chewing motion. Notice that when you swallow, your tongue pulls back in your mouth a little. It's this sort of swallowing or chewing motion that's welcome because it indicates relaxation. When the horse chews or chomps at the bit rapidly, like chewing up hard candy, that's bad and unwelcome.

14

Fear

Fear is an instinct given to us for self-preservation. Somehow, people have come to think of fear as the antithesis of bravery; and as a result, they either are ashamed because they experience it, or refuse to admit that they feel it. A person who really and truly doesn't know what fear is can get himself into a peck of trouble.

Most people who handle horses all their lives will sooner or later experience some degree of fear of them. Most of this should be defined as respect; and when green riders mingle with more experienced ones, they are constantly being reminded to have respect for the horse: "Speak to your horse before you walk up behind him," etc.

The old-time California vaqueros had a saying: "A man won't make a good horse until he's afraid to ride." Freely translated, this means that as long as a man thinks he can stay on the back of a horse no matter what the horse does, he will never start using his head to train the horse to perform well. So fear — in this case meaning healthy respect of the physical powers of the horse — is essential to good horsemanship.

Plenty of people are afraid of horses because they lack experience in handling them or even in being around them at all. Those who have a love for horses and a determination to learn about them will lose this fear as they gain experience. Some, however, will not be so lucky. They'll get their first experiences with young or spoiled horses and find those experiences so painful, physically and emotionally, that they give it all up as a bad job.

It is essential that a person's first horse be gentle and well-

It is essential that the inexperienced rider and the fearful one have gentle, well-mannered horses that will build their confidence.

mannered. The better way to go is to take lessons, but that can get a person in trouble, too. If the school horses pull such tricks as bucking and flat-out running away, you'd better choose another place of instruction. If the horses simply take advantage of you to go where they please in the walk or trot, that's no trouble. You are there to learn how to control the horse. And don't think that that frisky colt or spoiled beauty you own will become a horseman's dream if you take your lessons on him. It is possible, but not probable, since you need months and months of practice under the proper instruction to be able to control yourself well enough to control him. All green riders should ride gentle, well-mannered horses.

So we have the fear that is respect and the fear that comes from inexperience. The third kind of fear — traumatic fear — can happen to anyone. It has happened to the green rider who decides he has had enough bad experiences. It can also happen to highly experienced riders. It happened to me about 35 years ago, and in the last 10 years I have thanked God again and again that it did. If a person hasn't experienced traumatic fear, he can't understand it. If he can't understand it, he can't help other victims. In fact, the only thing the fearless person knows to say is, "There's no reason to be afraid. Don't be so stupid." Or, "You might as well quit riding."

Traumatic fear is beyond the person's control. The event that triggered my fear was the time a colt bucked and fell with me. I wasn't seriously hurt physically but was badly damaged psychologically in relation to starting colts. Still, I couldn't give up, so many's the one I mounted literally trembling uncontrollably in my boots and singing, "God Will Take Care of Thee." The reason I'm "confessing my sins" to you is so you will understand that I understand and so you will know that my advice is sound.

I don't know that a person who has become traumatically fearful can ever overcome it completely. There are times when I'm tired and my spirits are low that I just don't want to get on a horse that's giving its rider trouble. Most of the time I can go ahead and ride the horse, and start curing its problem. There are some horses I refuse to get on — but I think everyone else should, too. Generally speaking, my fear is cured and I can tell you how it came about.

Within the last 10 years I was lucky to get acquainted with people interested in dressage riding and in bringing in highly qualified instructors for clinics. This isn't to say that dressage is the only cure for this difficulty. I found it one very good way to help, however, because it is one of the safest ways to ride a horse and because it is one of the most demanding in mental application and riding discipline. When you have to concentrate on using the correct aids and making the horse go forward properly, you don't have time for fears to surface.

At the first such clinic, I rode in a group lesson. In the middle of the lesson, our instructor ordered us to cross our stirrups over to ride without using them — if we felt secure enough to do so. That "if" let me off the hook until he called me by name to repeat the order. Half an hour later our class was dismissed and I rode out to my trailer. As I started to put my weight in the left stirrup to dismount, I almost fell off — there wasn't any stirrup there! I would never have ridden that spunky Arab out of the arena with no stirrups if I had remembered. Even though I hadn't fallen off a horse in years, this was a bigger breakthrough for me psychologically than all the arguments I had handed myself about riding ability.

If you are afraid, whether because of inexperience or because of psychological damage to your confidence, the first thing to do is admit it quite frankly. Keep in mind that anyone who sneers at you for being afraid is either too dumb to be respectful of a horse or has qualms himself and is too proud to admit it.

While I never got any direct sneers myself, I have been told that I was stupid to be afraid because all that could happen was that I might fall off. Some reassurance! Some people have even argued with me that I *couldn't* be afraid (because of my pre-established riding ability). Because of the maniac horse a new friend was riding, I myself was skeptical when she confessed fear. It's legend around here that she's under God's special care because of the wild horses she has owned and ridden without coming to any physical harm. Now she is overcoming both her fear and her gentler horses' occasional disobediences — proof of the soundness of the advice I am about to give you.

The best way to start is by taking lessons if you can find an instructor who is understanding and safety-conscious. This can be hard to do. Get permission to watch the person teach. Make sure the school horses are well-mannered or use your own horse if he is gentle and fairly obedient. Choose an instructor who is firm but uses more words of praise than condemnation. Choose one who is demanding of work at your level but not demanding of instant perfection. I have found both group and private lessons helpful, but you may find that one works better for you than the other.

If you own a horse that scares you badly, you should sell it and look for one that gives you confidence — one that *you* can han-

An understanding, firm instructor can help you overcome your fears.

dle. If your horse scares you only occasionally, and that by nothing serious such as bucking or running away, you might consider keeping him. Understand that your wanting to keep that disobedient horse is a matter of pride, not horse sense. Proverbs 16:18 states, "Pride goeth before destruction, and an haughty spirit before a fall." Being too proud to admit defeat on one horse can cause you to suffer total defeat.

It is always said that when you are afraid, the horse senses it and takes advantage of you. Any horse will take advantage of his rider when he can get away with it. It is true that horses sense fear. What this does to the horse is to make him fearful. He starts getting nervous and suspicious of things he would normally ignore. He is looking for the thing that you are sending out danger signals about and is prepared to protect himself by whatever horse means are at his disposal.

Any horse will take advantage of any person who isn't definite with his commands. Where there is a conflict of interest, the horse takes advantage of his rider's indecision. All other cases are because he doesn't understand your message. Even if you are so scared that you actually quake, you can learn to control the message you transmit to the horse and to be definite in your commands. Just having to concentrate on these can help you overcome your fear.

You can control your subconscious message to the horse by being matter-of-fact at all times. If you are continually whisper-

Approaching your horse hesitantly can make him nervous or resentful. Tahnya and Faysaan perform for the camera while Tyke directs from the sidelines.

Always handle your horse in a relaxed, quiet, matter-of-fact manner to give him confidence in you. This will help you to develop confidence in yourself.

ing "Whoa, boy" and approaching him hesitantly on tiptoe, he will start looking for potential trouble. If you try to make yourself believe that you are bigger than he is by shouting at him, he will hear your fear and frustration and become apprehensive of you as well as his surroundings. If you strike at him physically for no reason except that you are afraid, he will be afraid of you and may even reach the point of striking back.

Listen to yourself and watch yourself so that in spite of your fears you talk in a conversational tone of voice and move as if you're confident that you are with a trusted friend. Train yourself to relax your muscles. You can do this training while lying in bed, driving your car, or having a coffee break. Start at the top with your neck, then your shoulders, arms, hands, waist, buttocks, thighs, ankles, and finally your feet. Let each one "melt down" in order. You will find that your ability to consciously relax yourself is useful in all sorts of daily situations as well as in working with your horse.

Your goal is to be able to sit on the horse with all your weight down into the saddle and your feet just resting on the stirrups. If you raise your shoulders, clamp your elbows, take a death grip on the reins, grip with your knees, and push hard on your stirrups, you are tense from head to toe. Riding along in the walk, start at the top and relax each part of yourself downward to your feet. Become aware of tension so you can relax it wherever it shows up. Practice breathing in rhythm with the horse's strides.

Slumping in the saddle can help as long as you don't make it a habit. The proper and safest posture is to sit erect but relaxed.

Whether you take riding lessons or not, you need to do a lot of riding at home. It is best to have a fenced area for this. The round corral would do nicely, but you will need a larger lot soon. If funds are scarce, a fence of steel T-posts and old garden hose will work nicely. We put old tennis balls on the tops of the posts for safety. A good size for a riding area is 60' by 120'. It's big enough to get the horse moving when you want and small enough to help control him. Place markers of some sort on the perimeter, about three to a side and one at each end. Use something that you can see easily but that won't flutter and spook the horse. (Lots of people like to use plastic cones.)

You must think positive. Thinking "I won't be scared today" is negative thinking. Imagining the horse pulling a cute trick is definitely negative. Replace all negative thinking with a definite, premeditated plan: "Today I will ride in the walk six times around the lot going to the left. I will start at marker A and ride straight along the track. After six laps, I will turn to the left at marker A and ride six walking laps to the right on the track. I will stop at A and dismount." Ride your daily plan several times in your mind and then go do it on your horse.

In taking lessons you are told what to do and you concentrate on trying to do it. In riding on your own, you must be both the instructor and the pupil. Tell yourself where to ride and how to ride there and then see that you do it. Each day add a little more to your riding — stops, turns, trotting, and eventually cantering. Avoid routine in your figures but always make use of the markers so you have a definite place in mind for a change of gait or direction. If you use the same marker for the same thing each day, the horse will quickly learn the routine. You must ride the horse, not be a passenger on a guided tour.

Work first on being definite with your horse. If you plan to stop at a marker, tell him with definite aids and make him stop. Be both firm and matter-of-fact with him. Look ahead where you want to go and go there. As you get this more under control, start working on relaxing yourself; and when you are getting control of this, start concentrating on better rein and leg aids to

Letters for riding area markers are easy to make and are easier to use than "that rock" or "that post."

improve your riding. By concentrating on these things, you can build up your confidence.

Some days you won't want to ride at all. If you're terribly upset about something else, it can be a bad idea to ride because you might take it out on your horse. Sometimes you will find the concentration needed for riding a relief from other problems. At first your nerves will be able to stand just so much riding each day. Gradually you can push yourself a little farther by saying, "One more time around and then I'll stop." Always stop on a good note when your horse has obeyed you and you are relaxed. This is good for both of you. Horses think about the end of the ride, so don't give your horse a chance to gloat for 23 hours over getting his own way or give yourself that period of time to worry over an upset. Take a deep breath; relax as you exhale; choose a marker and ride firmly forward to it. Then you can stop victorious.

Regular riding sessions with an understanding friend can be quite helpful to both of you even if you are both fearful or one of you is far more advanced. Besides the psychological support of having someone there "to pick you up," your concentration is improved by having someone reminding you to correct riding faults. One of my bad habits is collapsing my left side and this makes my horse fall through corners to the left. When I have a friend reminding me to sit up straight, I don't have to fall through so many corners before I remember why my horse isn't "mind ing" me. Even an interested non-rider can develop an eye for proper performance in both the rider and the horse and so be helpful as a riding coach. This in turn can greatly improve your riding and your confidence. The friend can also call out riding orders so you don't have to concentrate so much on remembering riding plans.

When things are going well and your confidence is improved, start riding out after your daily ride. Have a definite goal in mind here, too, such as that oak tree down the road a piece or taking that pretty trail nearby. I find that selecting the route in advance makes riding more pleasurable anyway, although I'm constantly exploring new trails on impulse and ending up in brush so thick a jackrabbit has trouble getting through. Indecision concerning the route to take can be transmitted to the horse in the form of indefinite aids; so if you aren't sure which fork of the trail you want to take, decisively stop your horse while you mentally flip a coin to make the choice. Tell your horse where you want him to go and when you want him to walk, trot, turn, and stop. You can enjoy the scenery without losing sight of the fact that you must be boss.

Remember — it isn't your fear but your nervous manner that makes your horse nervous. He can hear it in your voice, see it in your movements, and feel it in your body. Don't try to control your fear; work on controlling your expressions.

Remember — a horse doesn't take advantage of your fear. He takes advantage of indecision. Work to be firm, quiet, and matter-of-fact. You will not only be building confidence in yourself but also be training your horse so you can have confidence in him.

Remember — being afraid is no disgrace. It can be the gate to becoming a better horseman than the rider who has no need to learn to control a horse properly.

PART III

Problems on the Ground

*Train up a child
in the way he should go
and, when he is old,
he will not depart from it.*
— PROVERBS 22:6

15

Leading and Tying

Halter breaking the foal

After my daughter was born, the doctor asked me, "What are you going to do with this baby now that you have her?" Feeling that a dumb question deserves a smart-aleck answer, I said, "Put her in a corral." (Isn't that what happens to most babies sooner or later?) Actually, since the doctor didn't know me very well, he didn't know whether or not I was knowledgeable in the care and feeding of first-born infants; so it wasn't such a dumb question.

Too often I receive letters stating, "My mare had a foal five months ago and now I want to know how to get a halter on it. They're in a small lot with an electric fence, but I can't catch the foal." Before these people ever bred the mare they should have asked themselves what they were going to do with the foal when it arrived. I don't like to solve this sort of problem by mail. A person who has waited this long to train the foal and doesn't have any facility to contain it isn't going to be able to control it once he gets his hands on it.

I once let one of my Thoroughbred colts get about a month old before I got around to haltering him. I didn't have any trouble crowding him into the corner of the corral to get my arms around him, but then he went bucking down the fence with me hanging on for dear life, determined not to lose him. Suddenly I realized that I wasn't able to get my arm behind this big colt's rump so I had it across his back with a grip on his off flank. As soon as I let go of his flank, he stopped bucking and stood still. An inexperienced person would have been in a lot of trouble.

If you don't have a stall or small corral that will safely confine the mare and foal while you work with the foal, build one. It doesn't have to be fancy — a 12' x 12' corral with solid posts and board or horse-wire fencing will do fine. The fence should be at least five feet high, the boards 2" x 6" or 2" x 8", the wire mesh 2" x 4". The fencing should be on the inside of the posts and two of the posts should be available for tying the mare and foal.

I don't halter a newborn foal. A halter should never be left on a horse of any age because of the danger of getting it caught on something or the horse getting his foot caught in it. I don't start breaking a foal to lead until he is at least a week old. Up until that time his mother has to follow him around because he hasn't yet learned to follow her; besides that, the mare is too nervous over her foal while he is still so young and her anxious talking will make the foal harder to handle.

When the foal is old enough, lead the mare with the foal following into the stall or corral. Make sure the foal is following closely because you don't want to leave him frantically tearing around outside, wondering what became of his mama. He won't find the gate unless he goes through it with her. When both mare and foal are in the corral, lead the mare back out, keeping the foal in and keeping the mare held or tied on the other side of the fence where they can see each other. You want everybody to stay as quiet as possible.

Have the foal's halter, without a lead rope attached, tucked into your hip pocket or under your belt out of the way but where you can reach it with one hand. Quietly crowd the foal into a corner; and when you are sure you won't miss, grab him across his breast and around his rump with your arms as you push your body against his. It is important that you *don't let him get away* because that would just make him try harder to get free the next time. He may rear and jump around, but you can hold him by moving along with him as you restrain him with both arms and your body.

Each time the foal stands still, I relax my hold a little so he doesn't feel as if he's held in a vise and I rub him with my hands wherever I can without losing my position. When he has accepted my holding and rubbing him, I crowd him against the fence with his tail in a corner. There I can hold him with my arm in front and my body against his while I rub the halter on his neck and then carefully slip it up over his nose and buckle it on him. I wait for a moment when he isn't trying to escape and turn him loose in the corral to get used to having the halter on his head. If two of you are working on this project, one can hold the foal while the other halters him. The person haltering the foal should avoid approaching him full front view.

When the foal decides he can't get rid of the halter and that it isn't hurting him, lead the mare back into the corral with him. Again crowd the foal into the fence so you can snap the lead rope into his halter. Don't try to lead him yet; just let him follow by his mother's side as she is being led out of the corral. Go along with him just holding onto the rope. Sooner or later the foal will try to run ahead or lag behind. This gives you a chance to show him his limits.

The reason for leading a foal instead of just tying him up is to let him get the feel of being restricted without his feeling totally trapped. You can yield a little to him where a post can't. If you try to hold him solidly or try to pull him along, he will probably fight desperately. Some foals fight anyway, but try to hold and yield alternately without letting him drag you all over the place. As much as possible make use of his following the mare for the first day or two.

Don't let the foal get started running straight ahead of you.

Betty holds Roufus in position to slip the halter on him.

Foals often buck when they wear a halter for the first time.

Drop out to the side with some slack in the rope and then let him tighten it. This will turn his head to the side and you will be able to hold him. If he balks when you try to lead him, tug his head to one side or the other to get him to take a step to catch his balance. With a series of tugs this way but never tugging or pulling when he is moving, you can get him to lead. You can tug as he starts to stop to keep him moving, but a steady pull will only make him balk.

Even on the first day you may need to resort to a rump rope to encourage him to go forward. I like to use a 10-foot lead rope and just hold the end and the middle with my right hand to form a loop to drape behind the foal. That way I don't need so much equipment and I have it without delay when I need it. Use the rope draped behind the foal's rump, just above his hocks, with a tug and release. Don't use it to drag him forward. He is to learn to walk forward willingly, not lead like a sled. Tug to get him to step forward; tug to get him to walk up better. Never tug when he is doing okay.

Almost every foal will try to rear when he feels the halter tighten when he tries to go backward. And almost every person will pull on the rope to try to prevent his rearing and then to try to keep him from going over backward. When the foal threatens

Mark holds Roufus
properly while Betty
removes the halter after
the colt's first lesson in
being led. Having a helper
is a definite advantage.

to rear, yield on the rope and try to step to one side to pull
again to turn him. When he rears anyway, give him slack as he is
going up and chances are good he won't fall. Trying to prevent
his falling with a strong hold can make him go over violently;
and if there is anything in the way of his head, it can kill him.
That is why he should be led first out in the open in an area free
of big rocks and other such dangers.

When the foal has let you get up to him several times during
leading without a big fight and has let you rub him over his neck
and body without trying to bolt, you can end the lesson by re-
moving his halter. Hold him with your arms and make sure he is
quiet enough that you can remove it without his bolting free. If
you aren't sure you can manage this, take the mare and foal into
the corral where you can crowd him into the corner while re-
moving the halter. We try to avoid letting bad habits get started
— it's easier than curing them later.

The foal's daily lessons should continue this way with your
leading him more independently of his mother each day. When
he is leading well, tie the two of them up side by side and leave
them for an hour or so. As the foal gets older, you can gradually
tie and lead him out of sight of his dam. Always use equipment
that he can't break. If his mother won't stand tied, tie him up and

hold her nearby. She can teach him a bad habit if he sees her pull back.

If you are one of those people who has a big foal and you don't have any experience in catching and training one to lead, build your small corral so you have a safe place of confinement. Get the mare and foal used to being in it for a feeding each day. Then call in a horseman who is experienced and tactful. It is cheaper to pay to get that big foal trained to lead and tie than to get hurt trying to do it yourself.

Problems during leading and tying

Horses have several ways of plaguing people who are leading them. Some are nuisance-things such as crowding and biting. A horse may crowd close to his handler on occasions when he is scared of his surroundings. This is what he did as a foal to feel the protection of his mother. As long as this horse doesn't overpower me, I give him the comfort of body contact. The horse that is simply disrespectful, crowding me every time I lead him, needs training. I keep my right hand holding the lead rope up beside his neck and hit it a short jab with my fist each time he gets too

After the foal leads well, tie him up daily at a safe place near his mother to train him to stand tied.

The horse that has been trained to lead well, like Pat's mare, is a pleasure to handle.

close. If the horse is really bad, a smart crack across his front legs with a whip will get his attention and respect.

Biting during leading can be cured by holding a nail in your right fist so the sharp end protrudes beyond your knuckles. Keep your fist up beside the horse's muzzle about six inches away. Each time he tries to bite, he will run into that nail punishing himself instantly. Even without a nail you can let him run into your solid fist this same way, making him think he did it to himself. If you try to punch him for biting, you will always be too late and he may even make a game of it just as horses play sabers with their heads.

The horse that ignores you to walk on ahead or around you can be put in his place very quickly. Pretend to swing a left hook at him as hard as you can. Bring that fist right into his face, but *don't hit him.* In his language you have told him that you are boss and he must get back in line. Keeping him in line this way can help prevent crowding and biting.

Some horses are so disobedient that they don't give you a chance to show them who is boss this way. The horse cleverly turns his head away from you and takes off. Going straight away from you this way, the horse will always win. Handle him the same way I told you to handle the foal. Give him some slack;

Pretending to swing a left hook forcefully into the horse's face — without making contact — will convince him to stay respectfully beside you. (Don't try this on an overly sensitive horse.)

leap to one side; brace the rope across your hips; dig in your heels and lean back. If you aren't quick enough and strong enough to handle the situation this way, just reach forward to get some slack in the rope and then swing it very hard against his haunches. This will make him swing his haunches away from you and put him in position so you can finish pulling his head around. It is best to use a braided rope halter on such a horse.

The horse that rears and strikes while being led knows who is boss. Very young foals can learn this quickly under green handlers. This rearing is different from a foal's initial efforts to escape the lead rope and it requires immediate, severe action. Carry a six or seven foot whip. When the horse rears up, step to the side and slash him across his hind legs hard. One slash for each rear is sufficient since a second one would come as the horse is bringing his feet to the ground where you want him to keep them. Repeat the punishment each time he rears. When a horse rears and strikes or just rears as a means of defying you, he needs this cure regardless of his age. He doesn't need it if he is merely frightened.

It is never advisable to lead a horse by the halter only. If something happens to frighten him so he throws his head up, or you must lead him across something that makes him raise his head to balance himself, you can't give his head enough freedom.

You can stop even a big horse from running away from you if you drop out to the side and brace the lead rope across your hips.

Finding his head snubbed, he may panic and jerk loose. If you have no alternative, be sure to use a light touch so you aren't totally restricting the movement of his head. He will come along a lot better. Get a lead rope of sorts on him as soon as possible.

You can avoid creating a horse that won't stand tied by following a few simple rules. Never tie a horse with the reins. If something spooks him, he can easily break them. If you aren't sure that your horse is thoroughly broke to stand tied, always use a strong halter and lead rope and avoid snaps by tying the lead rope into the halter ring. If you must do something with a horse that might spook him into stepping back suddenly, untie him first so you can control him tactfully instead of risking his breaking loose. Avoid doing things such as spraying him in the face and then wondering why he pulled back.

Never tie a horse to something unstable such as a lawn chair or a ladder. Avoid tying the horse to a tree where he can walk around it and snub himself short. This can cause him to panic. And for the same reason always tie with about 18" of rope between the halter ring and a quick-release knot. Tie at about the height of the horse's withers. He must not be snubbed close or low, nor should he be left with enough rope to hang himself.

Don't assume that your trained horse will automatically accept

Never tie a horse with the reins, nor to a weak post, nor in a hazardous place.

crossties. Crossties should be attached to solid posts or trees that are eight to ten feet apart. The ropes should be attached at average wither height and should be long enough to be easily snapped together. Train the horse by snapping one of these into a side ring of the halter and your lead rope into the opposite side ring. This way you can give and take on the lead rope to help him learn the feel of being crosstied without putting him in a bind that would panic him.

Even the best trained horse can be spooked into pulling back hard enough to break the equipment. At the moment the rope or halter breaks, the horse will be numb to what has happened for a second or more. If you possibly can, walk, don't run, to his nearest shoulder in a casual but firm way to get hold of him so he won't realize he has broken loose. Don't scold or punish him. Remove whatever spooked him, replace the equipment, and tie him up again when he has calmed down. Talk to him in a matter-of-fact way about the whole matter.

Some horses, especially colts, will relieve the boredom of standing tied by chewing on anything within reach. Protect your equipment by keeping it out of his reach. You can cure him of chewing on the tie rope by sprinkling it with tabasco. Paint any wood within his reach with creosote or one of the products on the market for preventing chewing.

The horse that is an equine Houdini, untying every knot known to man, can be foiled by tying him where you can take a turn around the post you are tying him to and taking the end of the rope on to the next post to tie the knot (see photo, p. 199). You need a long enough tie rope and two posts or trees that are far enough apart that he can't reach the knot. This is also the best way to tie up a colt or a spoiled horse to halter break him. In that case the two posts should be at least eight feet apart so you can get to the knot to release it quickly if the horse gets in serious trouble.

Some horses stand poised for flight while you unbuckle the halter to turn them loose in the corral or pasture. While it may be a thrilling sight to see your horse gallop off into the sunset, it is a bad habit for him to develop, making him prone to break away too soon. It can also be dangerous since he could get overenthusiastic and kick at you as he takes off. For such a horse I hold the end of the lead rope around his neck, giving it several tugs to let him know I have hold of him. When the halter is unbuckled, I hold it on with one hand and the lead rope with the other, tugging a time or two on it as I remove the halter. When the horse isn't making a move to leave, I slip the lead rope off his neck. This training doesn't take long if you consistently turn the horse loose when he isn't trying to get loose.

Curing pullers

The worst problem of all, of course, is the horse that won't stand tied. The best way to cure this (if you are familiar with California equipment) is to use a rawhide bosal adjusted so the nosepiece is about six inches below the horse's eyes. With a bowline knot tie a strong rope *snug* in his throatlatch when his head is at rest. Run the end of the rope between the cheeks of the bosal at the heel knot and tie a half-hitch around both cheeks between the rope and the horse's jaw. This is to keep the heel from slipping off his chin, so tie it short enough to raise the heel knot up level with the nosepiece. Now tie the horse at wither height to a flawless willow limb that is about as thick as your forearm. Tie with about two feet of rope between the heel knot and the limb.

When the horse pulls back, the limb bends, lessening the resistance and so lessening the horse's desire to pull. When he relaxes his pulling, the limb exerts pressure to encourage him to step forward. He will get sore around his neck and nose; but remember, he is doing it to himself and he has to have discomfort, not just inability to break loose, in order to realize the complete futility of pulling back. Some people use an inner tube for this, which gives some of the flexibility of the willow tree but isn't quite as good.

If you don't have a willow tree or an inner tube, tie the horse to a stout post or tree in a safe place. If at all possible, take a turn around the post and tie the rope to another post as I have described, making sure the rope in between isn't where the horse can get a foot over it. If you don't have a heavy bosal, use a braided nylon or cotton halter, not a flat-strap or leather one. The halter should have some "bite" to it.

Another effective method is to put a stiff lass rope around the horse's body just back of the withers. The honda should hang downward at the middle of his body. Thread the end of the rope

If the confirmed puller is erratic in testing your strong equipment, sack him out (see p. 197) so he will pull once or twice and find out he is truly tied.

Khalshek stands quietly
after several tying lessons.

through the noseband of the halter, adjusting the body loop until
it is just snug and tying the lass rope to a solid post or big tree
where the horse can't go around to snub himself short. Use a
halter rope, too, tied the right length so the lass rope will take
hold first. Tie both ropes to the post at wither height. The lass
rope will tighten around the horse when he pulls back, biting in
far better than a cotton rope would. When the horse relaxes his
pull, the lass rope will immediately relax its bite, rewarding the
horse.

No matter what method you use for tying the horse, you must
leave him tied several hours a day — preferably all day — every
day until he is completely cured. The only time I would untie a
bad puller during his struggles is if he gets himself in such a bind
that he is in danger of breaking a leg or his neck or of choking to
death.

If your horse pulls back only occasionally or you want to make
sure he will no longer pull back, sack him out tactfully (see p.
197). In the first instance you want him to pull back in order to
get on with the lesson. In the latter case you just want him to
show you that he respects the rope enough not to set back on it,
so don't try to goose him into setting back regardless of his
learned respect.

Whatever tools you use, they must be strong — no snaps to
break — and severe enough that the horse doesn't care to experi-

Nona checks Khalshek to make sure she has learned her lesson well.

ence their bite continually. If you feel your horse is too valuable or you "love him too much" to let him suffer some swelling and abrasions, then you will just have to put up with having to stand and hold him wherever you go.

16

Trailer Loading

Training to avoid problems

Although feeding a horse in the trailer is one good way of teaching him to load, it can have some disadvantages. It ties up your trailer, or at least makes it quite inconvenient to use, since it must be blocked up front and rear to make it safe without its being hooked up to a towing vehicle. If the horse has an inquisitive mouth, all exposed wiring must be protected, plus any other chewable material. Not every horse that accepts the trailer as his manger will then load easily on command. And a distinct disadvantage is not having a trailer to feed him in.

When I acquired a herd of horses and was subsequently training the two-year-olds to load by feeding them one at a time in the trailer, the most nervous one walked right in for his feed the first time; yet he refused to load by hand after a week of eating in the trailer. A very gentle colt was nervous about going into the trailer on his own for feed but loaded on command with no trouble at all. The pet filly that had been mistakenly raised in a corral was so unconcerned about everything around her that she would complacently stand there eating like a cow chewing her cud, with everything but her hind feet in the short-box trailer. She was so insensitive that nothing would move her and I often threatened to put roller skates on her hind feet and haul her that way.

Even though this filly ran on my hilly pasture for a year before I broke her, she was still scary to ride because she seemed so ignorant. She would walk rapidly down steep, treacherous trails as if they were a paved road, and one time she would have walked right off an eight-foot drop if I hadn't stopped her. She wasn't mean or locoed, just uneducated to normal horse environment. It wasn't surprising the first time I hauled her to a friend's ranch for a ride that she refused to load to come home simply because she hadn't fully satisfied her curiosity. She willingly stepped partway in and then just stood there trying to see all those things she had missed exploring as a growing foal. I asked my daughter to hold the lead rope, picked up the only thing available — a 2 x 4 — and startled the filly with an unexpected tap on the buttocks. She let go a sigh and calmly walked on in.

Now I don't recommend a 2 x 4, but with a whip anyone can train a horse at home without a trailer so he can (with patience and understanding) load the horse when needed. It is just a case of gaining the horse's trust and of training him to go forward when tapped on top of his hips with the whip. Trust is very important in all things you do with a horse, since it is better to have a willing servant than a fearful slave.

I have found the method described by Henry Wynmalen in *Dressage* to be the best for teaching a horse to go forward when tapped with the whip. There are a couple of things that are important for you to understand about this method. One is that you are not leading the horse — you are walking beside him as he goes forward. The other is that the whip ultimately signals him to go forward when it is over his hips and must be removed from that vicinity when you want the horse to stop.

Stand beside the horse's girth facing the same direction he is facing. Hold the lead rope in your right hand with enough slack that you don't have contact with the horse's head and he can take a step forward without tightening the rope. Hold the balance of the rope and a willowy stick or whip in your left hand with the whip pointed up away from the horse. Lower the tip of the whip to the top of the horse's hips and tap once, easy; pause; tap again harder; pause; and so on until the horse takes a step. Immediately raise the whip and pet the horse. Repeat this until the horse will take a step forward when the whip is lowered to his hips.

Now lower the whip to the top of his hips and walk forward as the horse steps forward, tapping him as needed to keep him

Shirley is in position and ready to tap Misty on top of her hips to train her to step forward. (It's okay to hold the whip in your right hand if you prefer it that way.)

walking. Walk at his speed, being careful not to get ahead of his shoulder and using the whip to keep him ahead of you. When you want to stop, simply stop and brace your right arm as you raise the whip. If the horse is walking energetically, he will stop when he tightens the rope. Pet him and repeat this lesson. Remember: (1) you are walking forward with the horse; (2) the whip position is very important.

Often a horse will make circles around you. Give him enough slack that you don't pull on the halter; tap with the whip to get him moving faster; and walk fast enough to keep up with him. When you get the horse walking beside you with energy, he will walk straight ahead and stop straight when you stop. Avoid the temptation to lead him with the rope. You must be thorough in this training if you expect it to be useful in loading.

There is one other thing you can train your horse to do to make loading easier, but I hesitate to suggest it because it could be hazardous to you if your horse has any inclination to kick. Cure him of that first (I'll soon tell you how in Chapter 18) before going ahead with this training. When your horse is going forward well with the whip over his hips, put him in his stall by standing beside the doorway and asking him to walk in ahead of you, the way he will have to walk into a trailer as you stand to

Now that Misty understands, Shirley walks forward with her, using the whip position and taps, if necessary, to keep her moving.

one side behind it. This gets the horse used to going on ahead of you on command. Use a long enough lead rope that you can give him freedom by letting it slip through your hand as he goes into the stall.

Even for my well-trained horses I try to position the trailer to make it easier for them to get in and out. Proper positioning is absolutely essential if you hope to load a horse that won't. Taking care to position the trailer for easy unloading will help insure easier loading next time. I find a dip in the ground to drop the trailer wheels in, taking care that the back of the trailer extends over the higher ground. In positioning a ramp-loader, take as much slope as possible out of the ramp by dropping the trailer wheels in a dip. Make sure the end of the ramp rests solidly on the ground so there will be no give or tilt to it. All ramps should have some sort of non-skid strips across them to keep the horse from slipping.

I am very particular to avoid tilting the trailer so it is lower in front. If a step-in trailer is tilted this way the horse has great difficulty swinging forward over his front foot to take the second step into the trailer. Even with a ramp he will be reluctant to load downhill to the manger. Although a horse will load best if the front of the trailer is slightly higher, he doesn't like to ride in a

Putting a non-kicking
horse in the stall this way
is a big help in its
trailer-loading training.

trailer that travels that way. Be very particular about your trailer hitch — both in its strength and in getting its height to match your trailer. If the trailer is fresh from the factory, put some horse manure in it before you try to load any horse in it so it will have the proper smell for him.

Proper attitude of handler

It is essential to have the proper attitude when loading a horse. You must be confident, matter-of-fact, and patient. If you are afraid you won't succeed, you will tend to coax and wheedle and lose the horse's respect. If you let any anxiety, anger, or frustration show, the horse will become nervous. If you even think that you must hurry, the horse will become reluctant. Horses hate to be rushed into anything. Horses that load easily until the day of the show are just catching your spirit of the thing. You are excited over the preparation and anticipation for showing, but the horse just knows that you are excited. When you go to load up for the show, put everything out of your mind except the habitual routine of loading. Load him as if nothing unusual is going on. The same goes for hauling him home. Give yourself and your horse a chance to stand around and relax; then load him in the same matter-of-fact way you would at home if you were going nowhere important.

You can't rush a horse into a trailer, hoping he will be loaded before he knows what is happening. Thinking that his momentum will carry him in before he can lock up his brakes is foolish. Don't even try to keep a horse walking forward when he wants to stop. Your chances of keeping him moving are almost nil and he will just find out you can't. Don't pet him for stopping but do let him inspect the trailer, and give him some slack so he is free to look, smell, and feel without being allowed to turn away. When he relaxes, it is time to tell him to step forward.

When a horse paws at the tailgate or floor of the trailer, he isn't refusing to get in; he's feeling the strange footing to see if it's safe. Naturally, I'm talking about a horse you're training. If your broke horse starts pawing on the trailer in which he's ridden many miles, he's just being a bit stubborn or telling you your driving needs improving or the floor needs replacing. Basically I want the horse to feel and see what he's getting into. For that reason I would never blindfold one in an attempt to load him. It may work sometimes, but usually it doesn't or it just scares the horse so he won't load again.

I don't usually try to coax a horse in with feed, either. Horses are very clever at stretching their necks out, eating the grain, and then backing off. I do put a little grain in the manger along with some hay. I do feed a very nervous horse a little handful of grain now and then to help relax him — giving it to him when he has made a move to go forward. The grain and hay in the manger are to reward the horse when he is loaded and to help him feel at home in the trailer.

Proper loading procedures

Here are the four "don'ts" of loading: (1) Don't use the lead rope to try to pull the horse into the trailer. (2) Don't let the horse turn his head away from the trailer. (3) Don't lead the horse away from the trailer to get a new start when he turns sideways or refuses to go in. (4) Don't pet him for refusing in any way,

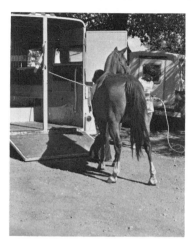

The horse's head must be in the trailer before you can control him to get him loaded.

thinking it will calm him. *Do* encourage the horse with kind words each time he offers to go forward.

Use the lead rope to keep the horse's head pointed into the trailer. If you try to pull him in with it, he will fight it, probably hurting himself and convincing himself that the trailer is as dangerous as he thought. Until the horse's head and half his neck are inside the trailer, you must help guide him by taking hold of the halter at times, because he can quickly put his head outside as he steps forward. This is why I like step-in trailers better — you can get the horse's head in the trailer before he balks at the footing. With a ramp you must patiently move him forward a step at a time until he is convinced the footing is okay. It is a big help if you have led him previously across things such as big sheets of plywood so it doesn't bother him.

I use a 20-foot rope with a panic (quick-release) snap for training all horses to load. I thread this rope through the tie ring, bringing the end out through the feed door to the back of the trailer so I can stand beside the horse to control his head and body. If the trailer doesn't have a feed door or an open side, you can bring the rope through the inside of the trailer on the side you will be standing, but it must be handled tactfully since its movement can scare some horses. Take up the slack on the lead rope without making it tight as the horse goes forward; brace on it so he pulls against it himself if he offers to step back.

Get everything ready before you bring the horse to the trailer — the hay and grain in the manger, the trailer properly positioned, the long lead rope installed with the snap within reach in the back of the trailer and the free end laid out straight with no kinks or coils. Never put your foot or arm through any kinks or coils of a rope attached to a horse or wrap the rope around your hand or arm, trying to get a better grip. Thumbs, fingers, and lives have been lost by ignoring this rule.

Lead the horse to the trailer with the whip and an ordinary lead rope just as you have trained him. Stop him at the back of the trailer while you drape the lead rope across his back and snap the long one into his halter and take up the slack. Stand beside the horse at the rear of the trailer and keep his head pointed into it. It is okay if he wants to feel the floor of the trailer with his lips or paw it with a foot but don't give in to him if he wants to turn away.

When you see the horse start to relax, raise the whip to the top of his hips and tell him to move forward. Use whatever voice command you habitually use and tap him with the whip as needed. Pay close attention to him so you don't tap as he actually

If your preliminary training is thorough, the horse will obey the whip and load. The long rope merely guides his head. The whip should be in your left hand, rope in right hand, when loading on this side.

Daniel also charged back out immediately. Use the whip, even with a smart rap, to keep such a horse loaded. You can't hold him with the rope.

steps forward and so you can take up the slack in the lead rope. Don't feel you must get loud with your voice and whip as he starts in to keep him moving forward to load quickly, while he is still moving. Remain calm and matter-of-fact. Some horses will walk right in. Others that are more apprehensive will have to make several starts to realize that it is safe and compulsory to load.

If the horse steps back, just brace the lead rope so he makes tension on it himself. There is no way that you can hold a horse that is determined to back out of a trailer, so let the rope slip some to avoid rope burn (you should wear gloves) and tap the horse on top of his hips if he steps back. If he quickly learns to step partway in and then charge back out, keep the whip poised over his hips, giving him a hard tap or series of hits if he charges back. He may charge out regardless, but he will probably stay in the next time if you keep the whip up in driving position where he can see it. You have trained the horse to go forward when the whip is over his hips. Use the whip as you trained him to load him and keep him loaded. Back off with the whip if he tries to go through the manger.

Most horses that are thoroughly trained to go forward with the whip on the hips will load with no trouble. Some of them may have already found out that you can't make them load. Tony was such a pony — a 13-hand stout one. His history of loading was, "He won't load so don't try." I had helped load him in a pickup

Keep the horse in the trailer with the whip over his hips while you snap the butt chain.

for a vacation trip, and his owners had completed the vacation with no more loading troubles. Later he was sold and I was hired to train him to load. In the meantime a girl had tried to load him, giving up when all he would do was step in and rear back out.

Tony was nervous about my handling him and about my trailer, so I was careful to show him he was in no danger. As soon as he realized he wouldn't be hurt, he started the rearing-back trick. Because I could see he wasn't scared any more but just deliberately using his strength against me, I took a dally with the long lead rope on the back of my trailer. He tried his rearing back, found he was held fast, gave up, and walked into the trailer. This procedure would panic lots of horses, but Tony was looking out for Number One so I knew it was safe with him.

Some horses can be told to go all the way in; some need to be convinced that they have to go in; some need to stop and relax in the middle of loading. If you try to convince a very nervous horse, he will reach the nervous breakdown point and refuse to load. If you don't convince the confident, overbearing one, he will use your sympathy against you. Successful horse handling is dependent upon your being able to read each horse's mind and manner.

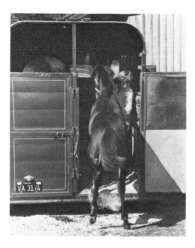

Pat uses patience and firmness to train her filly to unload properly.

17

Loading Problem Horses

Handling various problems

You don't always have time to train a horse to load — sometimes the job must be done right now. When that is the situation and the horse won't load, the job can be done with the right equipment and help. It isn't a case of forcing the horse into the trailer but of convincing him he can't go anywhere else. Over the years I have tried many different methods with varying degrees of success. The method I now use comes the closest to perfection but is handicapped by the need for knowledgeable help.

You will need two 20-foot ropes besides your long lead rope. You will also need two people who have some understanding of the way to handle those ropes with determination and tact or who will take orders. Position your trailer and your long lead rope and tie the other long ropes one to each side of the trailer at approximately the height of your chest. All of these ropes must be laid out with no kinks or coils and kept that way. Getting a hand or foot caught in a rope that is attached to a horse in any way can be fatal.

Lead the horse up to the trailer and attach the long lead rope, then step outside the other long rope on the loading side. The people handling the extra ropes can pick them up after the horse is at the trailer or before he is led up. Some horses see them held up and won't go up to the trailer; others need the ropes to form a lane to help get them close enough to hook up the lead rope.

The person holding the lead rope is to keep the slack out of it to keep the horse's head pointed in the right direction. The other two people put the horse in the trailer by crossing the ropes (called butt ropes) behind him, just above his hocks, and applying some pressure. This must be done tactfully, first to get the horse's head and neck inside the trailer and then to convince him that he should go on in. Certainly two fairly strong people can force the horse to load by putting all their weight into pulling those ropes, but this is foolish because the horse can fight it and get hurt — maybe even break a leg under the trailer or loading ramp. It is also very thoughtless, because somebody is going to want to load the horse again someday and he shouldn't have to contend with a badly frightened animal.

The butt ropes should be used to encourage the horse to step forward and to discourage him from going backward. I can't tell you how much pressure to use nor how long to apply it at a time. It takes different tugs for different plugs, so what you need is a repertoire of rope tricks and the ability to adapt them to the individual horse. Some horses are so leery of having the ropes behind them that they will walk on in without ever being touched. Some will sit on the ropes for a short time, then decide it is useless to resist and walk in without trouble. Others will stubbornly sit there seemingly forever. For those horses, try strong tugs followed by relaxing the pressure — either both ropes together or each one alternately. If that fails, one person can maintain tension while the other gives enough slack to flip his rope against the horse's buttocks.

Always let the tension on the butt ropes relax as the horse steps forward, just maintaining contact to be ready for any backward movement. To brace against the horse's weight, bring the rope across your loins and your outside hand around by your buttock. That way you can lean back to put your own weight into it. Never wrap the rope around your hips. I have had some horses take their own sweet time to load, but I haven't had a failure in years, except for one totally disobedient, totally disrespectful horse that thought the best escape route was over my dead body. With only half enough manpower and a trailer with an unsafe divider, I had to admit defeat on that one.

I have had a few horses kick when the butt ropes tightened. There is no danger if this happens, because you are working out of range. Just give to the force of the kick while maintaining

The two butt ropes are used to load the horse while the third helper takes up the slack in the lead rope.

constant contact and the horse will give it up. The people han-dling the ropes should wear gloves, but even then the way to prevent rope burns is to loosen your grip on the rope a little so it can slip. If the horse really wants to fight the ropes, you can't hold him through brute strength anyway — only through persis-tence — so gripping the rope to try to hold the horse will only take some of the hide off your hands as it does slip. Take care to keep the butt ropes just above the horse's hocks because a rope under the tail will make some horses kick wildly. Ropes below the hocks will give the horse's legs a rope burn and he can easily kick his way out of them.

This same loading method will work with just one long rope behind the horse, but two ropes are better because they prevent his turning sideways if the two people operating them pay atten-tion and keep the pressure even between them. One person can load a horse with the one butt rope tied to the opposite side of the trailer so he can operate the encouragement from behind and take up the slack in front as the horse steps forward. This can require more time and patience, but it is certainly better than nothing. Make sure those ropes don't pile up under your feet as the horse advances and you take up the slack front and rear.

When my friend Sara bought Tanjur and showed up with a covered trailer to haul him home, he refused to load, even though he supposedly loaded easily in an open trailer. The father of the seller unsuccessfully used every kind of force he could

One person can load a horse with the long lead rope and one butt rope. Have everything ready before bringing the horse to the trailer.

think of — mainly whipping and loss of temper — to try to load the horse. A couple of days later Sara located an open trailer and invited me to go along to help load Tanjur. He was scared of this one too, from the previous rough treatment, but we did manage to get him loaded. Later I had to load him in my trailer to haul him to my place, a job that took time and patience — and positioning the trailer so he had no place to go but in, once he had decided it wouldn't hurt him.

Sara asked me to train Tanjur to load better. Since he was so afraid of the trailer, I started out by feeding him his grain with his head barely inside the back of the trailer — that's as close as he would get. When he would finally stretch his neck as far as he could in order to reach the grain but still wouldn't voluntarily put a foot inside, it was time to load him. I attached a long rope to the opposite side of the trailer and laid it out in a semi-circle behind the trailer so I could reach the end of it. I led Tanjur up to the trailer, attached the long lead rope and picked up the butt rope. Because I had gained his trust and had shown him the trailer was really a pleasant place, he stepped ahead of the butt rope into the trailer. Because he was so nervous from his bad experience, we always used the butt rope to load him.

Later this poor horse was hauled by a young person who speeded down a twisty road, whipping around the curves and scaring Tanjur so badly that he reared into the manger; so when Sara had to move the horse to her new home, she called on me again. We didn't know what to expect, since no attempt had been made to load Tanjur in the few months since his latest bad experience. I carefully positioned my trailer that had always treated him so kindly, laid out the butt rope in its familiar place, and asked Sara to bring up her horse. As they approached the trailer, Tanjur took in the whole familiar situation and walked right into the trailer even though he showed signs of nervousness. The patient, thorough training had paid off. I drove extra carefully on that trip to reassure him that all was safe and secure.

Daniel was another horse that loaded well in an open truck but didn't want to get into a covered trailer. He also wouldn't stay there once he was in or back out without charging. When he came to me for other training, I was told that his owner's father had called on some of his fellow horsemen to help "train" Daniel to load. I discovered severe rope burns on both of Daniel's hind pasterns and — not surprisingly — that he still would not load consistently. After getting his trust, I taught him in one lesson to respond to the whip, to get into the trailer obediently, and to stay there until asked to back out and then back out slowly. Consistent use of the whip and long lead rope over a period of several weeks finally made Daniel a consistently well-mannered loader. The method you must use and the time you must spend depend on your horse's disposition and previous experiences. Always take your time, be thoughtful, and keep the rough do-it-yourselfers away. Show the horse it's safe to enter — not that it's painful to refuse.

Modern trailers with the fixed center post aren't conducive to loading. A horse doesn't care to go into a dead-end area that looks so narrow. These trailers also make it more difficult to load a horse that cleverly turns sideways to avoid going in. Never lead a sidewinder away to bring him back straight. This teaches him he can refuse and that turning sideways is an effective way to do it. If I whip-train a horse, I like to train him to move his hindquarters to each side on cue. In using only one butt rope with a fixed-post trailer, it is best to tie the rope to the center post to prevent this sideways escape.

If your horse gives you trouble loading, always prepare for the

Turning a horse's head loose before he's obedient gives him a chance to find out that he doesn't have to load.

worst until he is thoroughly obedient. If you don't know how a horse will load, prepare for the worst. If you have to stop trying to load him while you set up the equipment, he has got his own way — at least for a while — and will take longer to become obedient. Even when he begins to load well, still have the long lead rope on him for control while you teach him to go in by pointing his head into the trailer, throwing the short lead rope over his back, and telling him to get in. Turning a horse's head loose before he is obedient gives him a chance to find out that he doesn't have to obey.

Some horses will give you trouble backing out — either too fast or not at all. If the horse comes out too fast, use the whip on his hips to control him if you have whip-broke him. Otherwise tie a long rope to the opposite side of the trailer and brace yourself to hold it tight across the back of the trailer, just where it will catch the horse above his hocks. Attach the long lead rope so you can immediately put the horse back in, repeating this until he backs out slowly. Don't think you are going to actually stop him from rushing out — you will just slow him down — so bring him to a stop gradually, the way you apply the brakes on a car. Repeat this several times, and he will usually decide there is something back there to be cautious about.

On the other hand, always take your time closing the tail gate behind a horse. Train him to stay in the trailer. Let him know you are there. Remember your mother's constant reminder in the

The butt rope will stop him before he backs away from the trailer and will put him back into the trailer again immediately.

days of your youth — don't slam the door! You want the horse to be respectful, not scared into the manger.

Some horses are so impatient to get out that they sit on the butt chain. Use the whip to train them to step forward and stay forward while you unsnap the chain. For horses that won't back out at all, use your long lead rope fastened to the horse's halter and run it inside the trailer, directly out back beside the horse (next to the side of the trailer). Pull on this rope at the level of the horse's heels, keeping yourself to one side, out of danger. This pulls his head down and straight back so he can and must back out without trying to turn.

Drive carefully when you are towing horses. You can't stop as quickly with a trailer, so slow down to 55 on good roads, and go slower on poor ones. Whipping horses around corners and bouncing them over rough roads can make them reluctant to load. Hurrying to load a horse can make the best loader balky. Always load as if you have plenty of time even if you are late for your date. And remember, if you ride your horse abusively when you reach your destination, he is plenty smart enough to figure out that a ride in the trailer is like a trip to the dentist. Another thing that can make a horse associate the trailer with danger is backing him out into unexpected trouble. One man told me he got stuck crossing a stream and had to back his horse out into hock-deep water. If you absolutely can't avoid the problem, turn his head so he can see what is behind him before you back him

A smart tap with the whip can train a horse to stay forward until you unsnap the butt chain and ask him to back out.

out. Explain the situation to him. He may not understand your words, but he will understand your meaning. The horse that trusts you will also forgive you if you give him credit for more intelligence than he actually has.

Don't make a habit of hauling a horse with his saddle on. I saw one poor horse trying very hard to get in the trailer without success because the stirrup kept hanging up on the divider. If you

If the horse refuses to back out, pulling on the lead rope in this position accomplishes the feat.

must haul a horse saddled, tie the stirrups up; but remember, it doesn't take any longer to saddle the horse when you get there than it does to saddle at home. Always remove the bridle during hauling — sheriff's posses and horse opera heroes excepted.

If you habitually haul your horse on the same side of the trailer, you may be surprised one day to find out he won't load on the other side. This can put you in a bit of a bind if both horses you are trying to haul will load only on the same side. This shouldn't give you any trouble if you realize what's happening and if your horse is obedient and trusting, but it is a good idea to switch sides occasionally so you won't have this problem crop up.

You have to use judgment when loading unacquainted horses together. It is best to load the timid one first since the bold one in the trailer can very subtly — or openly — tell the timid one to stay out if he values his life. If the problem isn't one of who's boss but of one horse simply being nervous about loading, it can help him see that it is safe if the other horse is loaded first. If the strangers are a mare and a gelding, it is usually best to load the gelding first. A stallion and a mare can ride together with no problems if you hang a wool army blanket — no synthetics — between their heads. This blocks out smell as well as sight.

There are horses that literally try to climb the wall when they're being hauled. These scramblers have a balance problem and want foot room sideways to brace themselves. Try putting the horse on the opposite side of the trailer. If the divider goes all the way to the floor, shorten it so there are two or more feet of open space below it. If the horse still scrambles, you will find he rides okay alone with the divider removed so he can brace his hips in the opposite corner. Don't try to force him forward with the butt chain because that is too weak and unsteady for him.

When tying a horse in the trailer, give some thought to the length of rope. He needs to have his head free enough to help him balance. Some horses panic when they are snubbed down. Tie the rope long enough so the horse can raise his head comfortably. On the other hand, don't tie him so long that he can bend his head back around the divider or (if there is no divider) pester the other horse. Make a habit of tying the horse after the butt chain is snapped up and of untying him before it is unsnapped. If a horse tries to come out of a trailer while he is tied, he can hurt himself badly.

If your horse rushes backward out of the trailer and throws his head up in the process, it is best to put some kind of head protector on him while you are training him to come out like a gentleman. You can buy a padded head protector or use a thick piece of latex foam or a folded piece of blanket — anything you can tuck under the crown of the halter — during unloading. It not only protects the horse against sudden death, it encourages him to keep his head down better since it feels to him as if a piece of the sky has already fallen.

Loading the suckling foal

It is foolish to try to haul an unweaned foal without his mother. It is also foolish to load the mother with the foal running loose, thinking he will go in to be with her. The foal just loses sight of his mother and starts screaming, and both of them get frantic. Always take both of them up to the trailer together. If it is a very young foal that you haven't haltered, one person can hold him in

This latex foam protector saved Tyke many a headache while he learned to step out of the trailer calmly. It is just a piece of foam you can slip under the crown of the halter, after the halter is on the horse.

position at the back of the trailer by standing directly behind the foal and wrapping his arms around the foal's breast. Two people can hold a bigger foal by standing one on each side and locking their hands behind him.

You can keep a halter-broke foal headed into the trailer by having the person behind him use the long lead rope threaded through the tie ring and brought back inside the trailer. While the foal is held in place by whatever method, the person leading the mare should load her in the trailer. Then the person — or persons — who are holding the foal can gradually crowd him forward until he gets in. Take a little time to do it; don't try to slam him in like a bag of beans.

There is always a certain amount of risk involved in handling mares and foals. The people handling them should work quietly but confidently to minimize the risk of getting kicked. When you must work behind them, stay as close as possible and keep talking in a matter-of-fact way. A kick at close range isn't usually damaging even though it can be painful.

When hauling small foals, I take the divider out so the foal can turn around and ride backward. My tail gate was low enough that I was afraid a nervous foal might try to jump out — although it turned out that one never tried — so I had three pieces of chain welded on each side of the top so I could snap in a stall guard for safety. I wouldn't haul a loose foal in an open trailer. Larger foals will usually ride quite contentedly headed forward. Leave the

Steve holds the foal in place while Mary loads the mother. No ropes are needed on a very young foal.

This big filly's first loading. It took effort but I held her in place until she stepped in. Out of sight at her feed door, Pat guided her head with a long lead rope.

divider in place and tie the foal if he is trained to tie. Otherwise leave him loose. He's with his mother in a snug stall and therefore quite contented — unless your driving scares him.

If you will remember that a horse must put a lot of trust in you to go into a trailer in the first place and that he is completely at your mercy while in there, you will begin to develop the attitude needed to solve most of your trailering problems.

18

Vices on the Ground

I have no use for a horse that kicks, bites, or strikes. If I own such a horse, I find a way to cure him of his nasty habits. Any horse may do one or all of these things at some time in his life. When you bring home that gentle horse that you just bought, he is quite likely to start biting and could possibly kick or strike under the right circumstances. This is defensive behavior because of his apprehension over being in a new environment. I bought Pi Dough as a two-year-old stallion. When I was loading him in the trailer to bring him home, his breeder said, "There isn't a kick in him." At his new home he turned out to be quite a kicker — not vicious, but kicking out at anything unexpected behind him. The breeder didn't lie — Pi Dough simply was scared.

Dos was always a touchy horse who needed a gentle hand in grooming. One day I forgot this and started scrub-brushing some dirt off at his elbow. His hind foot flashed forward, barely brushing my arm. My reaction was instant — I swatted him on the shoulder with the back of the brush. Then I realized he had a right to react somehow because I had hurt him, but I wasn't about to feel sorry I had swatted him, because any horse I handle must learn to express himself in a much more tactful manner.

Causes of aggressiveness

The main cause of aggressive behavior in a horse is unjust punishment. This may be in the form of jerking on the horse's mouth, riding him too hard, asking him to perform strenuously beyond his level of training, or riding him when he has sore spots

— all things done thoughtlessly by riders who think they love horses. Then there are the riders whose philosophy is to make the horse afraid because they feel that the only safe and obedient horse is the one that is scared to twitch an ear for fear of punishment. Most horses resign themselves to all of these forms of mistreatment, but there are some horses that have the will power to fight back so they become aggressive.

Another cause of aggressiveness can lie at the door of the timid or incompetent rider. When you stop to think about it, you can't term a horse lazy just because he prefers not to run barrels, jump fences, and travel for miles on steep trails; but we do put that label on him because we have to train him to do these things obediently and willingly. If the timid or incompetent person lets a horse get away with a slight disobedience such as laying back his ears and refusing to leave the barn, the horse may push it farther and farther until he finds that all he has to do is lay his ears back and act as if he will rear or kick and his owner will let him rest in peace. Then he's labeled mean and ornery instead of just lazy.

So when you blow all the chaff away, you get down to two kernels of truth — the horse that habitually bites, kicks, or strikes at you does so either for fear of, or because of, unjust punishment or because he has learned that you aren't capable of making him get off welfare and go to work to earn his oats.

Biting

Biting is perhaps a more serious problem than kicking by virtue of its frequency. A mature stallion is able to pick up a man in his teeth and toss him several feet. Foals, like children, seem to put everything in their mouths, including people. Ponies can be expert biters.

A horse naturally bites as part of defense, offense, lovemaking, and social chitchat. It's interesting to watch a horse search out a particular area on his buddy to chew so his buddy will know which part he himself wants chewed. It's fun to watch horses playing sabers — sparring with their heads and nipping as if trying to find the opening for one lethal bite. The stallion often bites the mare during lovemaking; horses of all sexes bite to

Horses bite for many reasons, including offense, defense, and roughhouse play.

prevent an invasion of territory or to instigate such an invasion of their own. Mares bite their foals as a means of disciplining them.

Horses can bite people for any of these natural reasons. Ponies are often sparring with you or may be establishing a pecking order. Horses and ponies that bite at you when you approach them with the halter may be telling you that your riding is causing them discomfort. Some horses are protective of their mangers or shading-up spots and let you know you are invading their privacy by threatening to bite or kick. Mares are especially good at biting over rough cinching since biting a rough-nursing foal is second nature to them. While you shouldn't let your horse get away with such behavior, you should examine the way you handle him to determine if his protest is justified.

I have had two different horses bite me affectionately. In both cases I reacted immediately with horrible yells (this sort of love I don't need!) but then I thought it over and realized they weren't trying to get me. Swede could have taken my whole thumb off and Daniel could have easily ventilated my ribs. Neither horse hurt me in the least, but the thing that told me they weren't being nasty was the way their heads came around to take the bite. A horse that is trying to take a chunk out of you will swing his head quite suddenly and threateningly. Both of these horses brought their heads around the way you would reach out to pat someone on the shoulder — which is why they actually got their teeth on me. Even though I felt badly about discouraging their signs of affection, I certainly didn't apologize for my reactions. Having a horse think of you as another horse has its disadvantages as well as its advantages.

Yelling loudly and suddenly is a good way to discourage a horse from biting. A horse has sensitive ears; he understands the extreme threat in your voice; he connects the punishment with the crime; and he doesn't become headshy. Swatting at a horse's head for biting is almost always too late and is often an invitation to him to play sabers with your fist. If he takes it for the punishment intended, he doesn't know what the punishment is for and will become afraid of your hand when it's raised for any reason.

Less startling to the horse than ear-splitting screams is having your elbow or fist in the line of fire so the horse runs into it as he tries to bite and thus punishes himself. This makes the punishment automatically timed just right and prevents the horse from thinking that your hand or arm is a weapon at all times. I told you how to keep your nailed fist close to his muzzle during leading (see p. 161). During any work beside a biter, such as saddling, keep your elbow up. It is advisable to wear a denim jacket so the horse will still punish himself without danger of hurting your elbow; although if you have sharp elbows like mine, he's bound to be the one that suffers. You can watch out of

Leading the biter with the "nailed" fist in place. (Iam doesn't bite. I bribed him with a carrot!)

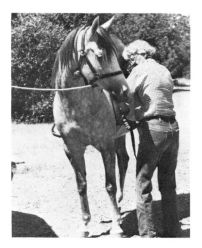

Keep your elbow in the line of fire at times when your horse habitually tries to bite. It provides instant punishment without making the horse headshy.

the corner of your eye so you can make sure it's your elbow that connects.

We are always told not to hand-feed horses because it makes them bite. Horses of Pi Dough's nature can get quite demanding and grabby. It is best not to hand-feed goodies to this kind unless you are quite confident around them. I have had Pi Dough get hold of a finger by mistake. How he knows the difference between that and a piece of carrot, I don't know; but I've never had him mistakenly bite down on it.

On the other hand, through hand-feeding I inadvertently cured one horse of constantly trying to bite me. Red Cloud had been abused by several people (including a woman) so he defensively bit at me when I came too close to his stall. The handful of grain I fed him whenever I milked the goat in the adjoining stall convinced him that I was to be trusted and stopped him from trying to bite me. I don't recommend this cure, though.

Striking

The horse that rears and strikes at you or strikes with one foot as you stand holding him is being aggressive. It may be because you have teased him in some way or because you have timidly let him get away with such behavior. Regardless of the cause, he needs immediate, severe punishment with the whip — on his hind legs for rearing and striking, and on his front legs for striking with one foot. You should, however, be aware of one thing — many horses will strike as if in panic at a fly buzzing under their chins or around their front legs.

The horse that strikes at a fly (real or imaginary) has a valid excuse. In earlier days my gentle yearling filly struck me in the head because I stuck it under her nose where a bot fly was bugging her. I don't think she knew she hit me and I didn't know it either until the blood got past my ear. It sounded like a thump on a wooden drum — which says something for my head — and I thought she had hit the fence post. That accident was due to a collision course. Don't stand directly in front of a horse during fly season. Don't poke any horse in the muzzle with a finger even with the intent of petting him.

Sacking out the horse

The principle of curing kicking is quite basic. It is to get the horse to understand that most things don't hurt him enough to warrant kicking and, if necessary, that he who kicks, gets kicked. Most kicking is inspired by some action of the handler, past or present. Just startling a horse or cornering a scared one can provoke him to kick. Thoughtless riding can make him threaten to kick to avoid being haltered for handling. Neglecting to discipline a threat to kick puts the onus on the handler — not the horse.

I sack out the kicker. I want to emphasize that this does *not* mean scaring a horse into submission. This business of tying up a horse and coming at him with all the scariest things you can think of is one of the most horrible things you can do to a horse. Sacking out simply means gradually getting the horse used to things that aren't part of his normal environment — things that he must encounter during his daily use. I sack out all horses I work with in order to make them safer to ride and to be around.

When you rub your hands on a horse, you are sacking him out. When you brush him, use a wipe rag on him, blanket and saddle him, carry a sack on him — anything you do that is unnatural to a horse is sacking him out. The important thing is to do it properly — to start at the beginning and to work up to the scary things and to avoid pushing the horse into a panic.

The first thing is to have the horse under control. Tie him up with a strong halter — nylon or braided cotton — and a strong rope tied into the halter ring. Tie him with a quick-release knot to a strong post or tree in a safe place. All this is just a precaution because you can't always tell when to slow down to keep the horse from pulling back. A safe place is a post in a heavy board or pole fence at least five feet high or beside the solid wall of a barn or shed. You don't want the horse running around the post and snubbing himself up short. Tie him at about wither height with about 18 inches of rope between the halter and post.

If a horse is very ticklish or touchy, you must start out by simply rubbing your hands on him or brushing him. If he's used to all these things, you can start out with a burlap feed sack. Let the horse smell it and then start rubbing it on his shoulder, up his neck a ways and on his body. As he accepts that, flap it on his back and under his belly. To flap it down his hind legs tie it to a stick so you don't get within kicking range. Sack out both sides of the horse.

From the feed sack you can go to noisy things like chaps, but avoid plastic for a while as it is especially scary. Use your lead rope or a lass rope and flip it around his front legs and then his

The purpose of sacking out a horse is to get the horse accustomed to things, not to scare him into submission. The low forks of this tree are dangerous if you are inexperienced at sacking out.

hind legs. You can do this without hitting him. Drag it on the ground beside him and wiggle it on his back, neck, and haunches. If he kicks at the sack or rope, maintain a steady flap, flap to get him over this reaction. Always go easier in sacking out the horse's head, rubbing — never flapping — and always approach his head from the side.

All of this can take a week to a month depending on the horse. It is very important that you don't panic him. You can push him a little when he's scared, but watch his expression so you can stop and reassure him before he gets scared enough to jump around frantically. If he is leery but not on the verge of panic, a monotonous flap, flap, flap of the sack against his body will get him relaxed more quickly than stop-and-start again and again. You can decrease and increase the force of the flap as needed. Anything such as flyspray, a water hose, or clippers can become commonplace to a horse if it is run steadily beside him and isn't turned on him suddenly when he least expects it.

Kicking

This sacking out, if done properly, can cure the horse that is inclined to kick first and see what's there second. Start from the beginning and be thorough. Don't just start out sacking out his hind legs, even though you will want to concentrate more on

Gentle repetition teaches the horse he can safely leave his foot on the ground, that he doesn't need to kick. (Note the slip knot tied to the tree where I can safely untie it in case of an emergency. See p. 165.)

them. Eventually you can even drop things behind him unexpectedly and he will do no more than flinch. Even then, don't stand within range to do this. The horse might be more asleep than you thought and react without thinking.

I cured Pi Dough of kicking by tying a three-foot rope to one corner of a gunny sack and tying the rope to his tail. I had him in a 20' x 30' corral and turned him loose with this sack dragging just barely within kicking reach. Poor Pi Dough! He had just reached the point of realizing that kicking that sack with his off hind foot did absolutely no good and certainly didn't hurt him any when he turned his head to the left to discover "another" sack following him. However, it didn't take him long to accept it on that side, too.

Three days of about six hours a day of dragging that sack and he was permanently cured of kicking. But I don't recommend this procedure for just anyone. You have to be able to put the thing on the horse securely (I used a sheet bend in his tail) and safely. You have to be able to judge whether the horse is being scared beyond reason and then get such a horse out of it safely. However, it is a thing that works very effectively on some horses.

To show you how well this cure worked on Pi Dough — a month or so later I was holding him on grass and my ten-year-old son was on a board fence near us. He wanted to jump down and I told him to go ahead since there was plenty of room between us if he had just dropped down. Instead he jumped with

A hard swat to the belly will punish a horse for kicking. (This is only a demonstration. Iam doesn't kick.)

The horse that threateningly turns his rump needs a hard swat on same with the end of your rope. Don't be easy or he might kick back.

such force that he tipped forward on his hands when he hit the ground. That put his head in ideal kicking range behind Pi Dough. The pony didn't even flinch, but I nearly had a heart attack, cursed my stupidity, and thanked the Lord.

Besides sacking out, there are other things to do in just generally handling the horse to teach him not to kick. If he swishes his tail in your face in an obviously well-aimed hit, speak sharply to him, "Cut it out!" Speak gruffly like a sergeant, not a hysterical woman. If he kicks at you as you work beside him, slap him hard with the flat of your hand on his shoulder or the side of his belly. Don't be dainty or easy about it — be sudden enough and hard enough that he jumps away from you. Then in a matter-of-fact way go on about your work with him.

If your horse turns his rump to you when you enter his stall, hit him on the rump with the end of your rope. Repeat this each time he turns his rump until he will stand facing you as you approach his shoulder. In all cases check up on your riding and handling habits. A kicking horse doesn't need the cause — just the cure.

Iam acts fierce as we demonstrate how chasing gets started. It isn't wise to run from your horse even in play.

19

Chasing; Hard to Catch

Chasing

You have gone into the pasture to visit with that kind, gentle horse that you love and pet so much. You call him by name and his head goes up. You call again and suddenly he is coming toward you in a full gallop with mane and tail flying and hooves shaking the ground. In a seizure of fright you turn and run for the nearest fence, barely making it over as your horse comes to a sliding stop, head tossing, eyes shining, and front hooves stomping the ground. A bad habit is born.

What got into your kind, gentle horse? Why did he suddenly chase you out of the pasture? He came galloping toward you because he was in an exuberant mood and was glad to see you and hoping you would play with him. He chased you out of the pasture because you ran. Horses just naturally love to chase things; in fact some of them will take off after anything that will run. It isn't necessarily a sign of meanness, although I have heard of horses that are very seriously bent on destruction in their chasing. I always wonder what happened to them to make them that way.

A horse charging straight at a person is enough to frighten the bravest soul. Frightened or not, if you know the horse, there is only one thing to do and that is *stand your ground*. When the horse is within 50 or 60 feet of you, suddenly start waving your arms like a windmill, jumping up and down like a kangaroo, and shouting like a banshee. The moment the horse veers off or starts to stop, stand quietly, repeating the performance only if needed. A bad habit is nipped in the bud. Don't try this on a strange horse that comes after you for no apparent reason, unless you are caught out in the middle of nowhere. He could be very badly spoiled.

One time I had corralled a yearling filly while waiting for her buyer to take delivery. Even though the corral was large, two or three days of confinement built up plenty of excess energy in her, and she started charging up and rearing each time I brought her hay. Even though I stood my ground and she never offered to strike at me, this was a form of play that had to stop. I didn't want to sting her with a whip (even though that would have been just punishment), but still I needed something easy to carry in one hand. That's when I thought of the ordinary house broom.

For two feedings now that filly had reared at me. What fun! At the third feeding, as she towered above me, a big, hairy thing suddenly hit her full force on her side. The fun was over. I carried the broom for several more feedings just to make sure, but I never had to use it again.

I have used the broom on several such bold colts with complete success. I swing as hard as I can at any part of the horse except his head. The bristles won't hurt him, but they certainly teach him respect. More times than not I have missed the horse completely and I still got the needed results. The broom is light-

Linda holds the broom in a non-threatening position as she walks up to Pi Dough.

weight to carry; you can hold it pointed behind you in order to approach a horse without scaring him into being hard to catch, and you can deliver instant punishment if needed. I think because it doesn't hurt him — just scares him a little — it makes him respectful instead of resentful.

Another tool I have found useful in the chasing situation is a coiled lass rope. Just throw the whole handful of coils at the horse. They will rattle quite satisfactorily as they hit. Your lead rope, with or without the halter, will work too; but you must be careful to miss the horse's head since the snaps and rings could injure his eyes. I have used clods of dirt and leafy tree branches but never rocks or sticks. Just remember that a horse can't chase you if you don't run, and he won't chase you if you sound and look like a horse-eating monster to him.

Hard to catch

In order to handle and ride a horse first you must catch him. The first mistake a person can make when his horse walks away from him is to pursue the horse. There is no way you can outrun or outmaneuver a loose horse. The second mistake is to give up without succeeding, and the third mistake is to turn him loose again with no preparation for recapture. Even if you just put a halter and short drag rope on him, it is better than nothing, although this is a poor practice because of the danger of his getting the halter or rope caught in a dangerous way.

The first thing to do when a horse moves away from you is to stop. Even an easy-to-catch horse sometimes takes a notion not to be caught. Pi Dough is such a horse, and when he does move off, I just stop, look him squarely in the eye with my best schoolmarm glare, and firmly tell him, "Ho!" This is the only time I look a horse squarely in the eye — when I want to command his obedience through eye contact. If you stop when the horse moves off, he probably won't go more than a few strides. You can then size up the situation, position yourself to approach him from the side, and probably get up to him by being confident and matter-of-fact.

Horses can become quite clever at avoiding capture. In the days

Chasing a horse to try to catch him merely reinforces his playing hard-to-catch.

of running mustangs with horses, if a mustang escaped from the trap, the wise mustanger immediately abandoned that trap and built a new one at another location. Not only would the escapee evade the trap, he would tell all the other mustangs in the area about it so they could take a different trail when run.

Bill and I bought a band of Appaloosas from a ranch that had all the necessary corrals for a working range-cattle operation and well-trained horses to do the work. Yet shipment of those horses was delayed a week because it took their well-mounted men that long to corral one of the mares. She was very crafty and at our place would unobtrusively position herself so she could escape any time we approached any of the horses with a rope.

In another band of mares we bought (these were big ponies from an Arizona Indian tribe) was a Thoroughbred-looking black mare with saddle marks. If I stepped into the corral with the band with a lass rope, Nightmare Alice (who would kick, bite, and strike when caught) would immediately get in the middle of the bunch and keep her head down. Yet all you had to do to catch her was toss the rope across her neck or withers and she would stand still as if hogtied.

When my daughter was in high school, she lived at the school five days a week because it was too far for the school bus to pick her up daily. The mare that she owned at that time had been used hard at cattle work by her previous owner. Rusty would hang around the house for five days of the week, but Saturday and Sunday would find her taking her rest out of sight because those were not days of rest for her with Betty home. This mare had been thoroughly whip-trained in her youth and would stop dead in her tracks and wait to be caught if we threw a stick in her direction — even at 100 feet away.

These are some of the behavior patterns of hard-to-catch horses — those that have learned they can escape and those that have learned certain circumstances mean escape is impossible. Horses often use a lot of imagination in avoiding capture. Some industriously pick grass until you are within reach of them, then they suddenly head for a new patch of grass 20 feet away — again and again. Others wait to jerk away as you start to halter them. Dos would hide very quietly behind trees or brush. I admire their ingenuity in this endeavor.

A horse may not want to be caught simply because he would rather lead a natural life of eating, drinking, running, and resting. Usually, though, it's because he is ridden too hard or is jerked around and asked to perform beyond his ability. The reason he is hard to catch is because somebody somewhere along the line let him find out he could avoid capture. When you buy a new horse, don't turn him out to pasture immediately. He doesn't know you and trust you yet so he might play hard to get. Keep him corralled for a week or two while you get acquainted with each other, making sure you develop his trust in you during that time. Then when you turn him out, he's more likely to let you catch him.

A good practice with any horse is to halter him and tie him up every time you feed him — at least long enough for him to eat his grain. This way he learns to associate the halter with the feeding and may even learn to come to you when he sees it in your hand. I use pieces of carrot or apples the same way, going out to visit the horse when I don't want to catch him just so he associates me with goodies. I was recently criticized for this advice; my critic suggesting that the horse would be mad and never trust me again if I showed up without the carrot. In actual practice it just doesn't work that way. After the horse has learned to come — or wait for you — scratching him on the withers or where he itches will reward him enough to make him forgive you for forgetting the bribe.

If you must pasture your hard-to-catch horse, build a small corral in one corner of the pasture. It needn't be fancy — T-posts with old garden hose hung at the horse's elbow height will do. Wire a ring on the end of one piece of hose that can be slipped over a post to form a five- or six-foot gate. Go out every day to give your horse a cup or so of grain in a bucket or grain dish inside this corral. If he won't come in at first, give him the grain wherever you can get him to take it, even if you have to set the bucket down and back off. Gradually get him to come closer until he will go inside the catch pen for the grain.

When he will come in for the grain, close the gate, catch him, and brush him. Then lead him out and turn him loose. By doing this daily whether you ride him or not, you will get him in the habit of coming in for his handful of grain and brushing and you will have no trouble getting him when you want to ride. If you can't build such a pen, visit him daily to give him the grain anyway — or use carrots or apples. When he lets you get up to him to feed and pet him, start carrying a rope with you so he gets used to it always being there whether you catch him or not. Make time at least two days a week to catch him and groom him

Horses seem to know you are hiding that rope behind you and most of them will walk away from an extended hand.

Approach the shoulder of the horse confidently, carrying the rope on your arm. Avoid looking him in the eye as that can be quite unsettling to him.

even though you aren't going to ride him. Make being caught a pleasant experience, too.

There is a proper way to carry a rope when you approach a horse and there is a proper way to get it on him. A suspicious horse will be doubly wary when you hold one hand behind your back. Coil your rope neatly and hang it on your arm, keeping your forearm across your stomach. Let your other arm hang by your side. Horses seldom notice a lead rope even if it's white when you carry it this way. Having your hands in plain view and your arms hanging relaxed keeps the horse from feeling threatened. Always approach in a matter-of-fact way, never hesitantly or in a rush. You can be prepared to stop and look at the scenery if the horse starts to move away, and to move forward quietly when he stands.

Approach the horse from the side so you aren't driving him away or threatening his head. Aim to walk up to his shoulder and do so with your arms hanging relaxed, never with your hand extended. If you have to maneuver to maintain position, do so in a very calm, relaxed way. If you are poised to move in like a cutting horse, your body language tells the horse you are going to try to outmaneuver him. He's better at cutting than you are so don't challenge him to such a contest.

Never make a grab for a horse when you get up to him. When you get up to his shoulder, quietly start scratching him on his shoulder and work up to his withers. If he is the kind that will step away when you make this kind of move, slip your left hand across his breast and up his neck on the off side. The secret of holding a horse this way is to offer brief resistance each time he goes against your arm. If you try to hold him with a steady force, he will want to break loose and probably will.

When the horse relaxes, slip the end of the rope across his withers, pushing it over until you can reach your left hand under his neck to get hold of it. You can't hold a horse with the rope around the base of his neck but he won't notice it so much there, so continue to keep your movements calm and deliberate.

Holding the loop of the rope around the horse's neck, you can slide it up to his throatlatch, holding it there with one hand while you toss the coiled end out behind you to uncoil it. Never tie or snap that rope on the horse while the coils are on your arm or at your feet. Doing that could be the death of you. Now you can tie the rope around his neck with a bowline knot. Then you either lead him in or halter him if he is tricky about being led with just the rope. Trying to halter a wily horse to catch him can let him escape more easily. I always use the neck rope first.

Getting your hands on the freedom-loving horse is basically a psychological matter. For instance, you can make use of his instinctive curiosity or jealousy. If you ignore the horse and sit down nearby to braid a string out of the pasture grasses, his

The horse that jerks away from the rope will usually stand while you slide it across his neck near the withers, then work it up to his head.

When you have slipped
the rope up his neck,
hold him with it as you
toss the rope out straight.
Then tie the bowline knot
snug at his throat.

curiosity will get the best of him and he will come up to see what you are doing. If you pet another horse — and if that horse isn't boss over him — he will just have to come up to get petted himself.

Dos was a standoffish horse and somewhat hard to catch, staying just out of reach in a walk. When I was riding Coltburger, too, I would simply turn away and catch Burgic. Dos would watch jealously while I saddled and rode out on Burgie and would come to be caught for his ride when I got back home. While this might be breaking my own rule of not giving up until the horse is caught, it was still a psychologically sound move in Dos's case.

When I wasn't working Burgie, too, I would just walk Dos down. This is something you can do with any horse if you have all day and lots of patience. Just walk along calmly behind the horse, keeping a close watch on his movements. If he starts to break into a trot, slow down or stop briefly to let him get a slight distance ahead so he will feel he can walk. Try not to push him so hard that he breaks into a trot. When he swings his head to the right, take one step to the right as you walk along. When he swings it to the left, step to the left. This way the horse sees you

With patience and time you can walk a horse down by never crowding him and always appearing to be on both sides of him.

no matter which way he looks and becomes convinced you are on both sides at once. If you avoid crowding him into leaving the country but keep him walking and thinking you have him mostly surrounded, he will eventually give up and let you get up to him. I have done it in a big pasture and it has been done with wild horses on the open range — but the latter takes many, many days.

Some people have written that they can catch their horses with grain but don't want to do it that way. One girl was worried because she had to approach her horse on the off side to catch him. Any way you can catch your horse, use it. Be consistent, so you establish in his mind the feeling that being caught is the only option available to him. In all probability there will come a time when you will no longer have to be so careful in your methods.

If your horse is running in pasture with other horses, that can create a real problem. If you take grain out with you, the bolder horses will mob you while your horse stands on the outskirts drooling. If you try to separate your horse from the bunch, you will just stir them all up and your horse will follow his instincts to stay with them at any cost. I would take my horse out of that situation. You might as well not own a horse if you can't catch him. Put him somewhere else where you at least have a chance of teaching him to be caught.

One person wanted to know if she should punish her horse for running away from her when she finally caught him. Of course not — that's punishing him for being so foolish as to let himself be caught. Another practice that I detest is exercising a horse by chasing him around his corral or pasture with or without a whip. This can make a horse hard to catch and/or mean. Don't be lazy. Catch the horse and longe him or ride him to exercise him. One of the biggest factors in having a horse that's easy to catch is treating him with respect at all times.

Train your horse to pick up his foot, not just to *let* you pick it up. Bob, like all farriers, prefers shoeing the well-trained horses.

20

Problems in Handling

Picking up the horse's feet

The problems people have in picking up a horse's feet range from being kicked at if they attempt it to having the foot jerked away once it is up. If you have a horse that kicks at you when you try to do this, the first thing to do is cure him of kicking; then you can proceed with the training to get him to lift his feet. Keep in mind that you do train a horse to lift his foot, not to let you pick it up, although you will have to do some lifting in order to do the training.

Usually people don't have too much trouble with the front feet. Stand beside the horse on the near side facing his rear and lean your left shoulder into him as you run your left hand down the back side of his leg. As you lean into the horse to get him to shift his weight, pinch the big tendon at the top of his fetlock joint. Pinch with an upward movement and push your left elbow into the back of his knee. The combination of these three things makes the horse lift his foot. If at first it doesn't work, keep trying until you get the combination working. (Substitute "right" for "left" when picking up his off front foot.)

When the horse lifts his foot, be prepared to put your right hand under the hoof to hold it up. A horse doesn't like to have his foot left waving in thin air. Give his leg firm support and hold it so his cannon is parallel to the ground. You can rearrange your hands any way that suits you just so you do support his leg and foot where it is comfortable for him. When it is time to put it down, speak to your horse as you wiggle his leg a little to get his attention. As you then start to put it down, you should feel him

Pinch upward on the big tendon and push your elbow into the back of his knee to get a horse to lift his front foot.

take over and you can let it go. Do not try to put it down for him.

Never let a horse take his foot away from you if you can possibly help it. Each time he tries, bend his foot up firmly against his fetlock. When he relaxes, you can then hold it in normal position or let him put it down. Never just drop his foot without warning. This will make him distrust you and not want to lift his foot for you. There is one exception to this — the horse that leans heavily on you. Sometimes suddenly slipping out from under that horse to let him drop will cure him of leaning. Don't try this if you aren't nimble around horses because you could drop the horse on top of you.

Coltburger was the worst horse I ever had about refusing to pick up his hind feet. I will describe to you step-by-step how I trained him and that will cover almost any problem that you have run into in this area. He was good about his front feet so I started each lesson by picking up each front foot and rewarded him instantly with a piece of carrot. This helped establish in his mind the reason for the reward. He wouldn't kick unless unjustly punished but he would shift his weight to the hind foot I was trying to get up. This was the first thing I had to cure. I would simply stand beside him facing his rear and leaning my shoulder

When the horse lifts his hind foot straight up, slide your knee under his foot and walk it out back to a position that is comfortable for him.

into him until I felt him shift his weight. Then he got a piece of carrot.

The next step was to get him to cock his hind foot. For his left foot I leaned my left shoulder against his hip and ran my right hand down the back side of his leg. When he kept his weight shifted to the right, I tugged on the tendon just above the fetlock joint until he cocked his foot. Then he got another piece of carrot. The next step — I pulled his foot barely off the ground, held it for perhaps a second and set it down. Putting his foot down before he could take it away was as important as getting his foot off the ground. That way he knew I was in control.

Gradually I could get it higher, pulling it up and forward, and could hold it up longer. When he accepted this, I no longer pulled it forward but straight up and slid my knee under it for support. Eventually I could walk it out back to a position where it was comfortable for him.

All of this training took about two weeks, working twenty to thirty minutes daily. It also took several pounds of carrots because I always rewarded him for each little bit of progress. (Kind words are sufficient reward after training is completed.) I tried to be very consistent in being the one who put his foot down — at first before he could take it away and later when I held it long enough for him to relax. In a week or ten days I merely tightened my grip momentarily when he tried to take his foot, and he would respect that and let me hold it. When he did manage to jerk his foot away, I never punished him but just patiently went through the procedure to get it up again. *Note:* Don't mistake his jerking for kicking.

Several years later my horseshoer mentioned shoeing Burgie for his new owner. When I questioned him, he said Burgie was very good with his feet. Any of you can train your horse to pick up his feet this way. All of you owe it to your horseshoers to do so.

Saddling

It has always been my custom to start a colt in the fall when he is two and a half years old. I work with him for a month to get him quiet to saddle and bridle and to go out on the trail in the walk, trot, and canter under control. After this, I turn the colt loose to grow and strengthen and then catch him up in the spring for a refresher course and training.

Sandy was a very amenable colt, taking his sacking out and saddling very well and being very happy to behave like a gentleman out on the trail. The next spring I found I had to sell him; and since the buyer was a quiet-spoken cowboy who wanted the colt for his wife, I didn't think it was necessary to tell him how to handle Sandy. I just filled him in on the training the colt had had the previous fall and that he had not been ridden since.

A few days after taking the colt home the cowboy was back complaining that Sandy bucked and was very skittish when the saddle was thrown on him. He told me I should make a practice of throwing the saddle on colts so they would learn to stand for it. I was totally amazed. Here was a quiet man who earned his living using horses who thought that a month's work six months ago made the colt an old, broke saddle horse. My answer was direct and firm: "I never throw a saddle on any horse and no one else should either!"

Copying all this movie-TV cowboy stuff has ruined many

horses in all sorts of ways. While most horses seem to resign themselves to having the saddle thrown on them, some of them become downright paranoid about it. I don't cautiously ease a saddle on a horse after he accepts saddling, but I never heave it on with a big swing, off stirrup and cinch flying, and plop it down on a horse's back. This is the number one rule in preventing a horse's getting shy of saddling.

Some readers whose horses would not stand still for having a saddle put on their backs mentioned that they had even tried sneaking the saddle into place. Never try to sneak anything over on a horse. Think how you feel when somebody sneaks up behind you and pokes you. Always let the horse know you are there and what you intend to do. I know that a horse who is spoiled to saddle can be a lot of trouble. I one time placed the saddle on a horse's back a dozen times each day for a week to get him to accept that one thing.

Sacking out when done properly will help a horse accept having a saddle set on his back. Make sure the horse sees the saddle; let him smell it if necessary; rub it against his shoulder; set it on his back without a big heave and plop and without letting the stirrup and cinch bang him on the off side. Cinch up slowly by degrees. Pulling the cinch up with a jerk causes the horse discomfort by the suddenness of it and possibly by pulling his hair between the layers of latigo. This discomfort can make him hold a lung full of air or — worse yet — become cinchy.

Holding the off stirrup and the cinch as you lift the saddle onto the horse's back keeps them from bumping his off side.

Cinch up smoothly and by degrees to avoid making a horse "cinchy."

If your horse fills his lungs and holds the air during cinching, the worst thing you can do is slap or kick him in the belly thinking it will make him expel the air. He swells up like a toad because he has learned to be nervous about the cinching. Hitting him will just make him more nervous. It is better to take the time to let him stand just snugly cinched while you bridle him. If that isn't long enough for him to relax so you can take up more, lead him around for a minute or two. Make cinching as comfortable as possible — although I don't think anybody can enjoy being laced into a girdle of any sort.

The cinchy horse is even harder to handle. I have seen some that would stand perfectly still during cinching and for maybe a second afterward then suddenly throw themselves backward to the ground. I have seen a couple of horses suddenly drop to the ground, but this could have been from being cinched too tightly. Most cinchy horses simply pull back more or less. If you have a cinchy horse, always untie him to cinch him up; cinch up slowly and by degrees; walk him forward in between each time you take the cinch up. Never cinch any horse too tight — you should be able to slide your fingers under the girth or latigo. I cinch up all horses this way except for untying and walking them. That way I avoid making them cinchy.

After barely snugging the cinch, walk the cinchy horse to relax him before you tighten it more. The well-trained horse will lead behind you as well as beside you.

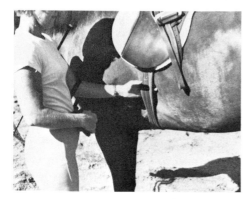

The properly adjusted cinch or girth lets you get the flat of your hand under it easily but snugly.

Use common-sense precautions to prevent accidents that would make a horse hard to saddle. Don't leave him standing around with the saddle uncinched or cinched so loosely it can easily slip to one side. Check your cinch for proper adjustment before mounting. If your saddle is double-rigged, always fasten the back cinch last and unfasten it first.

Bridling

While you can only observe the proper precautions in saddling the cinchy horse, you can retrain the hard-to-bridle horse. I started Swede in the hackamore but decided to switch him to the snaffle so I could ride him in dressage clinics. It was easy to bridle him the first time, but it was almost impossible the second. He was a long four-year-old and in putting my thumb in his mouth for the first bridling I had accidentally pressed his lip on his new, sharp tush. It took a month of patient work to get him to realize that bridling isn't painful.

To cure a horse of being hard to bridle you must understand the basic principles of bridling correctly. Never try to force a horse's head into position because this just makes him tense up and resist. Putting your forearm across his poll between his ears will get him to lower his head only if you just lay it there, tightening your muscles briefly to prevent his throwing it off. Using pressure will just make him raise his head higher. The same goes for keeping him from turning his head away. A brief resistance on the halter rope will show him his limits whereas a steady pull will make him pull harder. By the same token, don't try to keep his head down by snubbing him short.

Different folks use different hand holds in bridling, but one thing must never vary — the hand that holds the crown of the bridle lifts the bit into the horse's mouth and lowers it out of his mouth. The hand that holds the bit merely holds it in position so the other hand can raise or lower it in the proper place. If it is necessary to open the horse's mouth, insert the thumb of your bit-holding hand in the side of his mouth where there is a gap between his incisors and molars. Remember to avoid sharp tushes. Pushing your thumb up against the roof of his mouth is more effective than squeezing down with it.

Although accidents can happen, you should avoid hurting the horse both in bridling and unbridling. Never hurry through either process. Keep your eye on the horse's mouth so you know when it is safe to raise or lower the bit without bumping his teeth and so you can guide the bit with your other hand. When unbridling the horse, keep the hand that is not holding the crown on the horse's nose to coax him to keep his face in the vertical so the bit can fall free when he opens his mouth. Hold the bridle up until he does open his mouth or start spitting the bit out, otherwise he may spit it out suddenly letting it fall against his teeth. Don't crumple the horse's ears to get them under the crown when you

The curb chain wasn't loosened and the bit bumped Tyke's mouth. This sort of accident can make a horse hard to bridle.

The curb chain is now unhooked from the near side and Tyke accepts proper bridling.

bridle him. The best way is to slide the crown back past the horse's poll so it flattens his ears to his head, putting the crown forward into its proper place when the horse's ears pop up.

If you will observe all these rules in bridling and unbridling your horse, you may find you don't actually have a problem. If your horse takes the bit okay but panics about his ears, have them checked. If you have ever had an earache, you know how sensitive sore ears are. If he is just touchy about his ears or is headshy, you can cure him of these by rubbing him on the neck, working your way up toward the base of his ears. Again, don't try to force him to hold his head still but just offer brief resistance to let him learn his limits. Take as many training sessions as necessary to be able to rub closer and closer until he accepts handling on his head and ears. Always approach a horse's head with your hand from the side, never straight on.

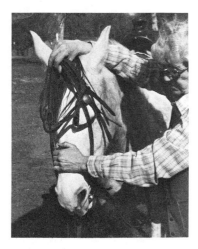

The hand holding the crown of the bridle raises and lowers the bit as the other hand guides it into place.

When you unbridle a horse, keep his face in the vertical with your free hand, to avoid bumping his teeth as you lower the bit by the crown of the bridle.

Bridling problems can be caused by something else besides improper bridling procedures, painful bridling and/or unbridling, or sore ears. The way you ride enters into it, too. If you are jerking on the horse's mouth a lot, he isn't too dumb to associate the pain with the bridle. And you can be sure he associates the bridle with painful riding.

You can train a horse to take the bridle easily with bribery. (The carrot growers should pay me a commission!) The worst bridling problems are the horses that panic at the sight of the bridle. These horses must first learn to take the pieces of carrot with the bridle held near them. By going step-by-step, feeding pieces of carrot to get the horse to accept each step in bridling in its proper order, you can teach the horse to relax and trust the bridling process.

Linda slips the crown of the bridle past Pi Dough's ears — the one time she can legitimately pin his ears back.

Bribery can work. I slipped the bit into Iam's mouth as he opened it for the carrot.

Some horses will reach for the carrot under the bit, so you can lift the bit into their mouths at that time. Others are clever at lipping the carrot into their mouths without opening up. The whole idea is to get the horse to relax and trust you to bridle him. Use patience and imagination. When he reaches the relaxed stage, you can bridle him and then reward him with the piece of carrot, eventually dispensing with it altogether. Never get careless. Save time by going slowly.

For those of you who are not very tall but have high-headed horses, this procedure will help train the horse to lower his head by getting him to reach down for the carrot. Those who have complained that their horses eat grass or hay or wander off during bridling should tie them up where there isn't any grass or hay.

Epilogue

In that day shall there be upon the bells of the horses, HOLINESS UNTO THE LORD.
      — ZECHARIAH 14:20

It is evident that horses will always be with us and that they are a very special gift. It always grieves me to hear a person angrily call his horse ornery. I sometimes call horses ornery myself, but not in anger. Knowing that the mistake is almost certainly the rider's makes one stop and consider how to approach the problem correctly.

A horse gets ornery through the way he is handled. Some years back the cover picture on a magazine was a colt with the question, "Will this colt be hard to break?" Out of curiosity I bought that copy to see what they had to say. I could tell at a glance that it would be a fairly easy job to start and train him, but what his handlers did to this colt in the name of sacking out and saddling made him into a frightened, frantic, fighting fool.

One of my students has a three-week-old colt and asked me what to do about his biting, striking, and kicking. Pursuing the problem, I found that he is quite gentlemanly while being led, but "ornery" when running loose. This colt should be running out in a big pasture with other mares and foals where he could take out his playfulness on his peers. Ideal conditions are not always available so I advised my student to take the house broom to him. Even though he is just playing with his own masculine roughness, he needs to learn that his human friends must be respected. His own mother won't let him get too rough with her.

From time to time the students in my classes are also students of my friends. It is quite interesting to hear my friends call some of these students' horses ornery. I ride the horses myself and find that their basic training has been wrong. They want to respond in the way that is habitual to them and so seem determined not to respond to proper aids. For sticking to their well-established habits, they are described as mean or having an evil disposition. Retraining a horse is far more difficult than starting him right, and the trainer must be far more tactful and patient. You can't force a horse to change in a matter of minutes.

Twice in teaching horses and their owners to longe I have had the horses charge me, rearing and striking. Although it was necessary to bring the whip across their hind legs as hard and quickly as possible to convince them I am not to be fooled with, it was obvious from watching their owners handle them why they behaved so badly. The yearling filly was spoiled like many only children; the three-year-old was spoiled from being handled much too roughly. Ignorance, manifesting itself in indulgence or severe punishment, makes far more ornery horses than bad breeding.

I have heard of horses that were born killers, but I have never met one. There is always a human factor somewhere in the soup. There are no problem horses — only problem riders.

Don't sidestep the issue: There are no problem horses — only problem riders.